Agent Revamp

How to Break Out of Your Real Estate Slump and Explode Your Income!

By Brett Miller

Cheri Alguire

and Eric Lofholm

Grow To Greatness Publishing

Printed in the United States of America

Cover Design & Book Layout by Brett Miller
Front Cover Photography © fotogestoeber – Fotolia.com
Back Cover Photography © Helder Almeida – Fotolia.com
Additional Images © GraphicStock, © AdobeStock (Krasimira Nevenova, cacaroot, Melpomene, Hannes Grobe, Melpomene, undrey, LoloStock, alexskopje, peshkova, aleksicze, GIS (Dollar Photo Club)

Miller, Brett / Alguire, Cheri / Lofholm, Eric / Agent Revamp: How to Break Out of Your Real Estate Slump and Explode Your Income!

ISBN: 0-9843323-1-6
ISBN-13: 978-0-9843323-1-1

1. Real Estate 2. Sales 3. Business

Published by Grow To Greatness Publishing
A Division of NLS Consulting, LLC
170 Rainbow Drive #7097
Livingston, TX 77399

www.AgentRevamp.com
www.GrowToGreatnessPublishing.com
www.CheriAlguire.com
www.EricLofholm.com

First Edition: January 2016

To every real estate professional with that entrepreneurial spark who has the dream of a successful life and the will to make it happen, you inspire us every single day and this book is dedicated to you.

CONTENTS

Introduction

Think back, for a moment, to the day you made the decision to become a Real Estate Agent. Why did you decide to go into Real Estate? What was it about this profession that intrigued you? Was it the money you could make? Was it the freedom it provided not having to answer to a boss? Or was it the flexible work schedule?

For me, Cheri Alguire, it was the possibility. I was in charge of my destiny, of how much money I made, of how many hours a week I worked and when I worked them. I could determine when I could take vacation time or if I wanted to work from home that day. I also loved the idea of getting paid to look at houses. How fun to go through house after house to find the best one for a client. What a rewarding way to make a living.

I didn't know, what I didn't know. I thought I understood the flip side of all these benefits I considered for becoming a Real Estate Agent, I didn't understand that becoming a Real Estate Agent meant I was starting my own business. I had to find my own clients and pay for my own advertising. I had to develop sales skills, presentation skills, and people skills. I had to manage me!

They say that 80% of agents won't make it. Most agents fail before they have made it to their two-year anniversary. Of those that do make it through those first two years, many are making so little that their income hardly raises them above the poverty line, let alone provides the financial freedom they are searching for.

How about you? Are you making good money, but spending too much of it on your business so that you end up with very little profit at the end of the year? Are you able to keep up with all the things you need to do to run your business from day to day? Do you feel pulled in too many directions?

How about that time freedom you are searching for?

Are you working the number of hours you want?

Are you taking off the time you want?

Are you able to work where you want and when you want?

Or... has your business taken over your personal or family time?

If you are reading this book, I bet you are looking for a better way. You know what is possible, you see those top agents who seem to have it all, financial success, purpose, balance, and the freedom to enjoy it.

Understand this: If you are a Real Estate Agent, you are a business owner. You may be a business of one, but you are running a business, not working in a sales career. Sales is definitely a part of it, and we even will go over one of the most important aspects of sales in this book, Sales Scripting, however, it is important as a business owner to figure out what you need to do to revamp your business to provide the success you are looking for.

You may have had some success up to this point; you may even be a top producing agent right now. We will build off of that all while examining what you can do to propel yourself and your business to the next level of success.

All three of the authors of this book are here to support you. We have helped to train, coach, and teach Real Estate Agents all across the North America how to become more, do more, and reach goals far above anything they ever dreamed.

This book will walk you through revamping your business. We will walk you through the practices that we have found will have the biggest impact on your business such as setting goals and creating a plan, going over the best online and offline marketing strategies, lead generation and lead conversion, helping you become the expert in your area by developing a platform, review what you should start doing, stop doing and what to delegate. Most importantly, we will introduce the one thing that will ultimately determine your success or failure in this industry.

We have taken brand new agents to a level of success many veterans are envious of, as well as taken top producers to superstar status. No matter what your goals are, what your background is, or what area you live in, you too can have the success you desire, as long as you are will to go through the process and revamp your business.

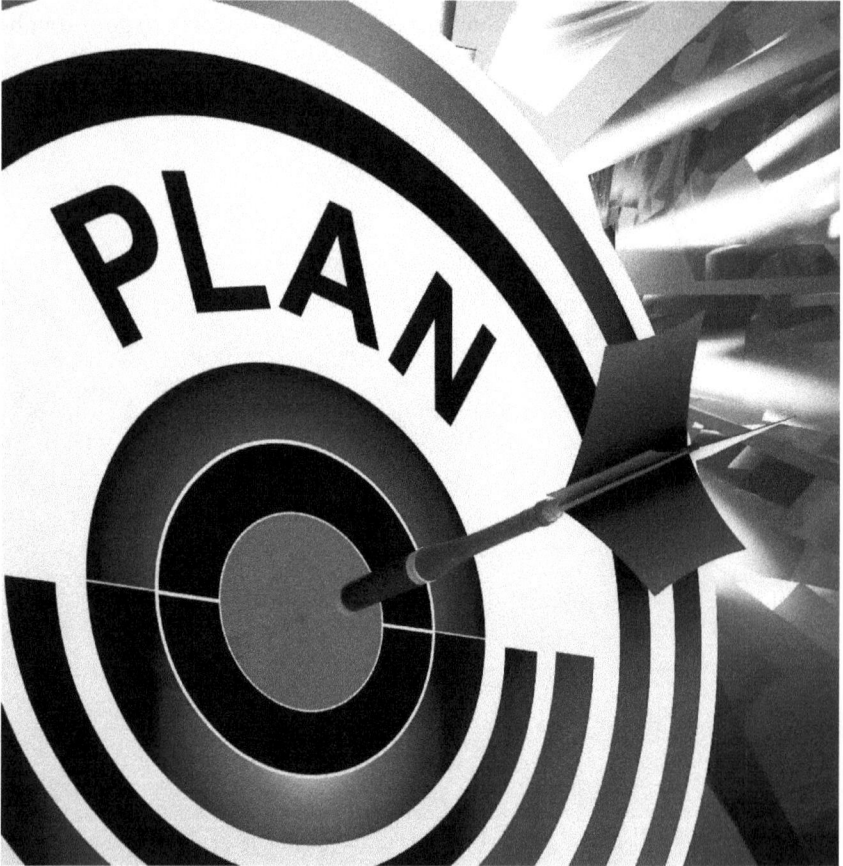

Setting Yourself Up For Success
With A Plan

If you are reading this book, it is because you want more from your Real Estate Business. You want to Revamp your Real Estate Business! You want more than you have right now. You want more from your business, you want more in life. Let's face it, you know you are capable of producing better results than you are currently producing, but you are just so busy with the day to day of real estate, that you are not even sure where to start.

This is where you start. Right here at the very beginning.

You start with making a decision.

A decision that you are tired of putting in lots of hours and not getting the results you want.

The decision that you are ready to refocus, regroup and revamp your Real Estate Business.

The decision that you are sick of playing small in life.

The decision that you are ready to go after everything you have dreamed of and desired.

The decision that NOW is that time for you.

Think back to a time in your life where you have accomplished something great. What did you do? How did you achieve that accomplishment? If you analyze your process, I will bet you followed this 3-step success formula:

1. You decided what you wanted exactly

2. You looked at where you were at the time, and then

3. You created a plan to bridge the gap.

That's it! It sounds so easy. Now, let's apply this same formula to your business.

What exactly do you want?

It sounds easy on the surface, but you want to create a goal that is going to worth it. You want it to give you the outcome you are looking for. However, you don't want it to be so big that it is unrealistic. You want to stretch yourself to live up to your full potential, but you need to believe you will get there as well. If you aim at nothing, you will hit it every time. We have all heard that we should set goals, but how?

Well, whether you realize it or not, the next five years will be a blur.... and when you get there you will either be asking yourself where the time went and bemoaning that you just didn't have the time to accomplish anything, or you can smile into the mirror with the realization that you took the time to plan out where you wanted to be and not only arrived there, but far surpassed your wildest imagination.

It can be done!

The power of this process is incredible. It all starts with a far-out goal, followed by a detailed plan of action. Then simply add in the baby steps it will take along the way and you're almost there.

I've designed a 17 part-planning workbook in response to the needs of many Real Estate Agents who have been awed by what they perceive as a near impossible task that goes into great detail on how to do this. As a bonus to your purchase of this Agent Revamp book, I have provided a link in the back of this book that will take you to a website where you can request the downloadable Business Planning Guide as well as access to three live recordings where I was walking a group of agents through the process. Let me summarize the process for you here.

It is important to set goals that are meaningful to you; goals that are really YOUR goals, not goals that are set for you by your broker or spouse. You also want to set goals that are the right size goals. Not too big, not too small, goals that stretch you out of your comfort zone, but not so big your subconscious mind doesn't believe you.

You must first figure out your WHY.

What do I mean by your WHY? Your WHY is the driving force behind your goals. Your WHY may be your family, or your kids. Maybe you want to provide a great lifestyle for your kids, you want to put them in private school, pay for the best colleges, or provide five star family vacations.

What is your purpose?

Purpose provides the foundation of our values, vision and goals. Purpose gives meaning to everything we do in our personal and professional lives, yet not all of us recognize our purpose or can articulate it. The following questions will help you uncover your purpose

Let's first talk about your life in general. What are the things that give you the most joy in your life? What are you most proud of having accomplished at this point in your life?

A "Purpose Statement" for your life is a few sentences that summarize your "WHY" for life. What really matters for YOU? What are YOU all about? What is your "Life Purpose Statement"?

Then we can focus in on your Real Estate Business. Have you had a time, professionally, in the past year when you have said, "This is why I do what I do everyday"? Describe that experience.

What do you offer that is unique or excites you?

A "Purpose Statement" for your business is a few sentences that describe the "WHY" you have a business in the real estate industry. If you are a real estate agent, you do have your own business in this industry. What is your purpose statement for your business?

Business and Life Purpose Statements can provide a basis for creating a vision and goals that are truly meaningful. They can also help drive us on a daily basis to do the things we need to do to reach our goals.

What are your values?

Your values are at the core of your personality and influence the way you respond to people and events. Your core values dictate what is important in both life and business: how business should be conducted, your view of humanity, and your role in society. Your core values are always at work in the background and are always present as a shaping force. They come from inside you and are an authentic extension of what you hold in your gut. Values direct and motivate us towards certain goals.

The first step in planning goals is figuring out who you really are, what is in your gut, so you can come up with goals that are in alignment with your core values. Not just regurgitate someone else's goals. We want goals that FIT!

Next, we will explore the process of creating the vision.

Sometimes life seems to get so busy and you are constantly working on the list of to-dos that you don't take the time to stop and evaluate your life. It is important to recognize everything you have done this year, celebrate the accomplishments and also look at what may have stopped you short of reaching a goal. This process will help you to learn from your successes and shortcomings and apply these lessons to achieving your long-term goals. What did you accomplish this year? What was challenging in this past year? What did you learn from going through these experiences of the past year?

Is your Life in Balance? Sometimes we focus our energies so much on a few areas of our life that we forget that other areas are also important. Which areas have you neglected recently? The Wheel of Life, sometimes called the Balance Wheel, will help you visualize your current situation. It will provide a snapshot of how you see your life today. Each spoke in the Balance Wheel represents an area in your life that can contribute to your feeling of happiness and satisfaction.

Now, you will NEVER be in total balance, however, it is important to acknowledge the areas of your life you may have been neglecting in pursuit of your other goals. If you wish, you can make the wheel more meaningful by changing any of the eight aspects given here. Give yourself a score based on your current level of satisfaction with each. This does not mean you are to grade yourself compared to others success based on society's ideals. This is about you and how you feel right now about your life. Rank the eight areas in the Wheel of Life on a scale of 1-10 (1 being completely dissatisfied and 10 being completely fulfilled)

1. Career/Business/Work   _____ (1-10)

2. Social/Friendships   _____ (1-10)

3. Community/Service/Charity   _____ (1-10)

4. Financial/Money/Lifestyle   _____ (1-10)

5. Physical/Fitness/Health   _____ (1-10)

6. Spiritual Growth   _____ (1-10)

7. Family/Love/Relationships   _____ (1-10)

8. Mental/Personal Growth   _____ (1-10)

If theses 8 areas were sections on a circular graph, or "wheel" and each was filled in on this graph based on your score, you would get a visual representation of how your life is balanced. How would your car travel if the wheels were in this shape? If half of the wheel is flat or if it is an odd shape and not round you will have problems gaining momentum in all areas of your life

What would you need to do in each of the 8 areas to raise the number in the next year? What are the 2-3 areas that if you improved, would make the biggest impact on your overall life? This exercise should be repeated at least quarterly to once again get this mental snapshot of which areas you may be neglecting and why you may be having trouble gaining momentum.

Next, we will begin to review what happened in your business this past year. Is Your Business Running Smoothly? Let's take that same overall process and break it down to your business. Just like in the previous exercise where we looked at your life overall, let's take some time to break down that first section call Career/Business/Work into 8 segments so we can really analyze how smoothly your business is running currently.

What is the shape?

What one, two or 3 areas could you concentrate on and make the biggest impact in your business?

Then it is time to begin Goal Setting! Write down every goal you hope to accomplish in the next year. Don't hold back, dream LARGE, think BIG, aim HIGH. Write out personal and Real Estate Goals. Writing them down is crucial. Your goals can't just be in your head. After you have done that, star the top 20%. 80% of your results will come from these top goals! Rewrite the goal in present tense as if you have already achieved it. Then write how you will feel when this goal is a reality.

Next, we will be looking specifically at your production goals in your business. We will work the numbers to find out how many clients you need to work with in order to reach not only your business goals, but the personal goals listed here as well. In order to hit the personal and general business goals, how does that break down into specific number goals for the next one to five years?

Once you have specific production goals set for the next 1-5 years you will begin creating the business and marketing plan to hit those goals.

Next we will be taking a closer look at your target market and how you are going to attract business from that niche.

Sometimes you choose your niche and it works out from the beginning. Other times, your niche evolves as you and your business change and grow. Remember, mass appeal equals no appeal. You can't be everything to everyone. Specialization gives people a reason to choose you. Specialization builds perceived value and being a specialist is also easier because you know your clients you can create systems so you can be more effective. Describe in detail your current niche: "Who" do you best relate to? And why? Who is your "ideal client"?

The money you make is in direct proportion to the Value you provide to the marketplace. When you are clear on your Value Proposition, your confidence will come across to every client and prospect you communication with.

Why should a prospect choose you as their agent?

What is your value proposition to buyers?

What is your value proposition to sellers?

I really want to stress the importance of doing this exercise. Be able to articulate your Unique Selling Proposition. This one thing alone can drastically change your business next year!

In order to attract your ideal clients to you, you must have an effective lead generation system and marketing plan in place. Earlier we looked at where you anticipated the leads for the sales you are projecting would come from. You need to create a marketing plan that will work in generating the leads from the sources you are projecting. It is important to recognize what specific changes to your current plans are necessary to make in order to reach your goals.

Describe your current lead generation system.

Describe your current Marketing Plan.

Create next year's Marketing Plan that can be broken down to a more specific "Editorial Calendar" Spreadsheet.

What changes are you going to have to make for next year in order to reach your goals? Be specific.

It is important to understand the Organizational Structure of your team. This includes team job descriptions and anticipated changes in the next few years.

Who is on your team?

Summarize their job descriptions.

Describe the compensation plans with those positions.

What changes do you expect to make in the next year?

In order to reach your goals next year, what changes do you need to make in specific areas of your business?

- A Development Plan will list the projects you will be working on throughout the year. This is the place to capture all of those things you have wanted to research, create, do, perfect, delegate and implement in your business. You may not have something for every area.

- Marketing and Lead Generation Systems (What kinds of systems do you need to bring in the leads, lead capture, database, social media, video, special reports, lead magnets, Referral of a Lifetime Plan, Relationship Marketing Plan)

- Sales and Servicing Systems (What kinds of systems do you need to convert and keep the leads, CRM, Top Producer, Auto responder, CardsForRealEstate.com)

- Equipment (i.e. Computers, printers, camera, Tablets, Smart Phones, Desks)

- Technology (i.e. Computer Programs, Websites, Internet Marketing, Social Media, HootSuite, Apps, SEO)

- People and Staffing (i.e. Assistant, Lead Buyer Agent, Transaction Coordinator, Marketing Manager)

- Support Systems (Coaching, Legal, Mentor, Social Media Management)

- Training - Self (i.e. NAR Conference, GRI, Real Estate Training Seminar, Personal Growth Seminar, Script Writing, Social Media Training, Internet Marketing)

- Training - Staff (i.e. Real Estate Training Seminar, Software Training, Team Retreat, Sales Training, Script Writing)

- Policies (i.e. Bonus Structures, Vacation Coverage, Policies for Buyer Agent Team or Administrative Staff)

- Procedures (i.e. Initial Lead Contact Procedure, File Coordination,

Consistent Incoming Phone Answering Procedure, Documentation of Procedures)

- Team Development (i.e. Adding positions, moving people within your team, increasing or setting minimum standards)

- Other (Anything else that you have wanted to do in your business, but have not implemented yet.)

Next, we will discuss budgeting and creating an Expenses Worksheet for next year. You will want to review your expenses for the current year and include any new marketing and development changes from the previous section.

Most budgeting and account software, such as QuickBooks, will provide reports for you to analyze your current business expenses and will assist you in creating a budget. If you do not have that type of system in place yet, you can use these charts in my Business Planning Guide to help you get started.

If you are not happy with these numbers, you may need to rework your development plan, marketing plan or production goals from previous sections. After you have total expenses, break them down to monthly expenses. This will be how you will use to monitor your expenses throughout the year.

Next we will break down your production goals even further.

In order to hit your business goals, you will need to break down a few of the key numbers down to quarterly and monthly goals: Number of Closed Transactions, Number of Buyer Sales, Number of Listing Sales and Number of New Listings for next year.

Break them down to Quarterly Goals and then Monthly based on your past sales trends. These Monthly Goals are what you will have to do and monitor on a monthly basis in order to hit your production goals next year.

This concept seems simple, but tracking these four numbers is KEY to a successful real estate business in the next year!

The final section of the Business Planning Guide will be to take everything and put it into a Master Project List that will break down all of your goals to specific next steps, breaking down goals and projects down to quarterly or monthly items that can be implemented and you can be held accountable to.

The Master Project List must be reviewed weekly with each action step actually scheduled into your calendar. Each week you will have new "next steps" that will need to be scheduled as well. As a result, your Master Project List will be a living document that will change, grow and evolve on a weekly basis.

Just completing this process does not complete your journey. You will need to constantly review and analyze your numbers, break down your next steps, schedule them and then do the things you know you need to do. This will be an ongoing process you will review and add to throughout the year as you hone in on completing each task on the road to achieving your goals.

The most important thing that you can do to reach these important life goals is to have an accountability partner or coach to help keep you focused and on-track so that "everyday life" doesn't creep up on you and rob you of this focus. Your old ways can distract you from the steps you need to take to propel you forward.

Big goals, when looked at in their entirety, can tend to be overwhelming. When whittled down into smaller, easy-to-digest steps, you will find yourself able to, bit by bit, finish up each individual project. By being consistent with following this plan, I have no doubt you will hit your goals, achieve your dreams and create an amazing year and life for yourself.

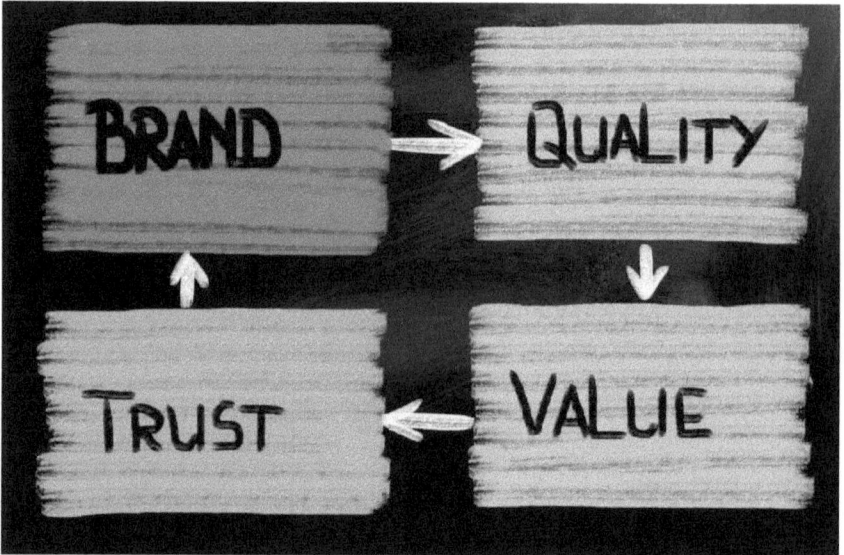

How To Present Yourself:

Your Brand

I have a question for you: Whose "Brand" are you building?

To be truly memorable and stick out in people's minds (and hearts) to become their top-of-mind Realtor, your personal real estate agent "brand" should be your own and authentic to you.

While we realize that you chose your brokerage carefully and that they are a great company, you are not required to market yourself exactly like everyone else in your office.

The fact is that YOU are your own independent entity and you have "hired" your brokerage to work for you. You've hired them to manage you, to offer workspace (sometimes) and a conference room for meeting clients, to provide regular training, to be the legal entity on record with listing homes, possibly act as your transaction coordinator, and ideally for offering valuable guidance along the way and be your mentor.

Certainly, when you are a brand new agent, there is much to learn from plugging into a well-oiled system that many Brokerages offer.

Another benefit of working with a Broker is that they often have marketing materials already created with their company brand all over them. You simply need to pop your little headshot into the right place, enter your contact info and voila, marketing done!

The business cards, brochures, and even personal websites are usually heavily discounted (if not free) and require next to no thought or planning… Just plug and play. Easy and cheap.

This may be okay for the newbie agent, but if you don't want to be perceived as a generic agent, and instead wish to raise your head up above the herd to get noticed, then you must step forward and invest in yourself to create your own unique brand.

When you do decide to step up and plant your flag, you should make sure you don't dilute your efforts by only using your brand in a couple of places and leaving your non-personal marketing in others.

For instance, don't create a personal logo, color scheme and design for yourself for your business cards and house fliers, and then continue to use your company branded website. This inconsistency will short circuit any good you have done for yourself in getting your brand in the first place.

(Obviously, you will need to follow the regulations and display your Broker logo in its proper place, but always in combination with your own agent logo.)

Your website especially needs to reflect you and your special qualities. In a recent report co-authored by the National Association of Realtors and Google, the report titled "The Digital House Hunt" (Google it) shows that fully 100% (yes, everyone) who buys a home is using the Internet now, up from the high 70's at the turn of the 21st century.

So, for you to be offering the same generic look and feel and offerings on your company-supplied website as everyone else in your office and associated brokerages nationwide makes you look generic and "just another agent." As Steve Jobs famously said, "Think Different."

USP – Unique Selling Proposition: Why is it Important and How to Craft it for Your Real Estate Business

The service you offer is great, but today's consumers want to know WHY they'd choose your greatness over the competition's awesomeness.

SO TELL THEM!

The Unique Selling Proposition — (a.k.a. unique selling point, or USP) was a concept in marketing proposed as a method to learn the pattern among advertising campaigns who made it to the top in the early 1940s. It states that such campaigns made unique propositions to the customer and that this made them switch brands.

A company's key points of difference are the same with its unique selling proposition (USP) although not interchangeable, and plays an important role in defining its competitive advantage and branding strategy. They must be characteristics that consumers strongly, uniquely, and positively relate to with the company's brand; and not with the competition. Once points of difference have been clearly dispersed to consumers, the consumers perceives the company and its brand as the one that stands out from the crowd.

What is your Unique Selling Proposition as a Realtor?

Why should I bring you my business? What do you have that others don't? Most people are too polite to ask these questions out loud. And if you don't tell them by way of your marketing, how will they know?

You know what you do, and you know what your qualifications are, but the consumer doesn't. And more likely than not, those that TELL the consumers what their strategy is and shows proof of HOW they can do it, has a great advantage over those who don't.

A very good example of an agent who does this is Angela May, the "Husker Home Finder." Angela's Omaha Homes for Sale website clearly spells out her "Selling Strategy" to get your home sold in no time. (Go this website: www.huskerhomefinder.com/sellers/ and see an example of a list of what she does and how she sells that to the customers.)

Here is an example:

> *I receive on-the-go messages on my mobile phone for web inquiries on your home, this means a quick response to all prospects!*

> *I hire an expert for all of my sellers giving them the tools to be sure they are way updated over our competition!*

I have a tailor fitted plan for each of my clients so we can achieve their goals in a timely manner.

How simple and easy can this be?

It all revolves on one simple question. Why does it have to be YOU?

Think of answers to this question and if you have them, then there's no reason why the customer would choose to go with someone else. This is an obvious part of any listing presentation and should be on your website and in the materials you send out to your prospects.

A great use for your Unique Selling Proposition is to turn it into a video for your website. In addition to that, here is another recommendation that will be worth your time; you can also turn your USP into a PowerPoint presentation, and create a computer screen capture video. With a headset and a PowerPoint presentation, you don't have to be in the video yourself, just your voice narrating your "marketing lines"! You can then upload that video to your YouTube account.

BONUS SEO TIP: Be sure to copy and paste in your entire "Selling Strategy" article into the YouTube video "Description" field area which has your contact information at the bottom. After you've saved your completed YouTube video, grab the "Embed" code from YouTube and post it on your homepage, webpage or blog post. Then you can share it on your Facebook, Twitter and Google+ profiles.

It is important to tell your prospect why they should choose you by creating your Unique Selling Proposition and using it everywhere.

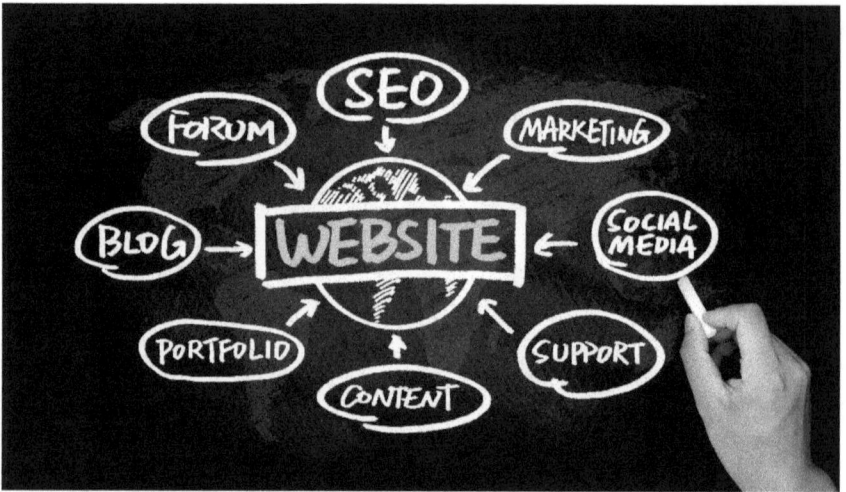

Your Website:

Cornerstone Of All Your Marketing

Why Using a Templated Website Hurts Your Business

If you're using a cheap, templated or broker-supplied website and are not getting any hits, there are some reasons that this may be. Search the Internet yourself to find out which Realtors like you are ranked at the top in different cities. How many of them are using a templated company-supplied site? My guess is not many.

Internet buyers and smart consumers have become a tech-savvy group. They've seen every type of small business website imaginable. When they hit a site that's obviously built on a boring template, they know it right away. Homebuyers searching the Internet have seen enough templated websites to know that such sites don't offer the personal attention they're looking for in your field, and their perception may be that these Agents don't have an original spark in their body.

Your templated site isn't generating any attention because it doesn't add anything of value to customers' lives. Having generic house photos on your site isn't going to drive you more business.

How can you fulfill all of your prospective clients' needs? What will you do that none of your competitors can or will do? It is necessary to answer all of these questions in your website and make them ask for more.

In a search engine world dominated by Google, one principal has become clear: Content Is King. The search engines regularly crawl through every website to see if there have been any changes since the last time they visited. If your site has added content since the last visit, you will be acknowledged as someone who has not let your site go dormant and seem abandoned.

If your site is templated with generic boilerplate copy that is exactly the same as a lot of other sites with only the contact information and your little headshot being different, you will all be given lesser value for being so similar.

This principal of search engines ignoring duplicated websites is especially true for company-supplied websites where everything is almost exactly the same. When that happens, no one ever has a chance of being found by potential clients that you have not personally directed to your site.

Regularly updated content that is rich with keywords relevant to what your site is about is important for showing the search engines that you are an important source of timely information. This is very important to the search engines. When your website is constantly updated, prospective clients know that it's not just a templated site. They will see that you are putting an effort into putting your best web-face forward, which is the key to marketing and sales strategies today.

A known fact is that the majority of today's consumers begin their searches on the Internet. If a website is difficult to navigate, or if visitors don't find their answers within the first few seconds of hitting a site, they'll leave as fast as they came. It must be click-click-click easy because you only have a few seconds to make a good first impression.

Your real estate website has to be a place that visitors want to come back to. A place where they know they can find information to help them achieve their goals. A place where you can build strong relationships with prospects and clients.

The best way to create such a place is with a personalized custom website that puts a human face on your business and doesn't look like you used a cookie-cutter approach for your business.

SoLoMo: Why Social, Local and Mobile are the 3 Most Important Elements of a Modern Real Estate Website

SOCIAL:

Are you wasting your daily mojo entering blurbs directly into Facebook and not using your own website as the repository for your thoughts and images?

Well, if so, Mark Zuckerburg needs to thank you for helping him get more SEO for his website at the expense of your own.

The thing is, according to Alexa.com's list of the top websites in the world Facebook is already #2 out more than a billion websites online today and Zuck really doesn't need your help. He's doing fine.

Maybe your website needs your help to get it higher ranking more than Facebook needs you to help theirs.

If you posted your local positive content about your area with photos, fun stories, positive life affirming stuff, all on your own website's Blog, then "Broadcast" your post to Facebook and Twitter with a link back to your site, you'd be showing Mr. Google what he wants to see.

Google follows every link through the social medias back to their home and then spiders the entire site. If your site consistently is adding new content (like new rooms on a house), Google will smile and kick you another step up their ladder. Don't disappoint Mr. Google. He can bring you a lot of business.

I saw a speaker in San Diego one time griping about people who wear other person's advertising on their clothes instead of promoting their own brand. While he went a little overboard (he was singling out a local guy wearing a San Diego Chargers jersey), his basic concept was sound:

Don't waste all your writing and inspirations on Social Media when you could plug that valuable content just as easily into a SoLoMo equipped website that will help you dominate your market.

A misconception is that you need to write something long and detailed like a magazine article. This is not true! In fact, this thinking will keep you from posting on a regular basis.

Not only do you not have time to write these articles, but nobody out there really has the time to read them.

Think quantity over quantity…short bursts like a Facebook post with an image done a few times a week in your own blog and broadcast to your Facebook and Twitter accounts. Bing bang boom.

The easier you make this, and the more fun, the more return you will get from your sphere who follow you and now who will remember you with a smile next time they are in a real estate state of mind.

LOCAL:

Having relevant local content is vital to being found by your target market. Google sees where you are searching from, and they really want to send you to the best site to answer your needs.

IMPORTANT: Posting local content doesn't mean linking to local city websites!

In fact, this is one of the worst things you can do. I see this all the time, real estate agent websites that link to the different local cities' web pages where all of their crime rates, poverty rates and negative data is there to read.

Plus, you're literally sending them away from your URL. This is totally not your goal!

Because you did that, Google will reward the other site by giving them better search engine ranking because YOU basically voted for that other site as being better than your own site.

Here's what you should be doing:

Think about the areas that you want to be the king or queen of, and regularly write about a different part of that area with a photo or two included. Even better, go to that location, pull out your smartphone's video-recorder and talk without looking at notes about what makes this area great for two minutes. Totally off the cuff from the heart.

Do not worry about style points! You being a perfectionist will mean this never gets done. Just do it and be real. Be enthusiastic. Simply love your area and be its biggest champion.

Don't think Entire Region, Think Micro-Target

Instead of focusing on making your site good for everyone in a 7-county radius or half your state, focus inward and really micro-target the specific housing developments and neighborhoods where your market is actually going to search for online. Create these pages one-at-a-time instead of all at once so you can show a regular drip-drip-drip of consistency with your posting. That's the kind of behavior that Google will reward you for.

A great local neighborhood page should have a paragraph that you've written yourself – in your voice – about what makes this a great place to live. This page should have a virtual map of any available homes for sale, some pre-searched links for easy clicking, a short embedded YouTube video of you riffing on what a great place this is, and some blog or news posts just about that neighborhood. If you focus solely on that neighborhood and nothing else, your page will be a great resource for Google to point to, and you could even redirect a custom domain to the same page if you wanted to target-market in that neighborhood.

Just having photos of houses on your site with no sense of love for the area will make you seem like an automated robot-site with no heart. Remember, people do business with people they know, like and trust. Decide that you will be that local agent with the positive outlook that makes people feel good when they visit your site or read your posts and not some generic boring nothing wallflower.

MOBILE:

In 2014, the "tipping point" for Mobile usage was reported when the total number of people viewing the Internet on mobile devices and tablets outnumbered those viewing on conventional computers. (As of this writing, Mobile now make up 60% of Internet users.)

This is a big deal. Google does not want to be irrelevant and be perceived as having "jumped the shark" by sending search results for a website to someone using a mobile device where the website can't be reasonably viewed on their smartphone.

April 21, 2015 marks the date now called "Mobilgeddon" when Google officially rolled out their mobile-friendly algorithm which would now give preferential treatment only to mobile-friendly "responsive" websites and start skipping over older non-mobile-friendly sites. In other words, Google will now only give good placement going forward to sites that offer a great Mobile experience.

That is why everybody who wants to still be seen and displayed by Google should invest in a responsive website.

Responsive is the term where your website looks good on any size mobile device, tablet or computer with the text all being readable and legible, and all of the elements of the website shifting automatically into a position that can be viewed on that device.

Imagine a couple out viewing homes for sale on the weekend. Is your mobile-optimized website the one they are using and loving, with the GPS built in to take them from house to house, or is your site ridiculously small on a smartphone where in order to read any of the text you have to keep using your thumbs to try to enlarge it and it never really works?

Or imagine that you have the indispensable local real estate website that feels like an "app" and where your loyal users can always go back to again and again.

What Elements Work Best for a Responsive Mobile Website?

1. Portrait and Landscape Viewing

Users are visiting your site on a plethora of different devices, all with all different sizes and proportions. They're also turning them sideways for a landscape effect or upright when portrait view is more effective for their needs. Your new real estate website should react automatically to the orientation of the device – not just to fill up their screen, but also to provide visitors with easy access to important information about you and your listings.

2. Making the Best Use of the Visible Area

"Real Estate" is also a term used for how much of the screen you're looking at is being used. You want to make sure your screen real estate is offering visitors all the main options without searching for them. A user searching for homes using his mobile device has less screen area to work with than someone using a iPad, Kindle Fire or other tablet. Great responsive sites adapt instantly to your users' needs based on the available screen size and viewing orientation when they're browsing.

3. Bigger Images Equal a Better Experience

Today's smartphones offer a full video and visual experience, and consumers expect it now. You need to deliver a media-rich experience. Make sure the images in your responsive real estate website are designed to "scale" to be as large as their mobile device will support. Large images draw in casual browsers and provide an easy way to link directly into the listing pages where they will get hooked.

4. Responsive Property Detail Pages

On a mobile device, your listing detail pages should show the addresses with photos up front to make it intuitive for prospective home buyers to click through easily and request more info from you. When displaying in a tablet, the home listing details pages should make it easy and fun to browse through all the photos, sideshows and galleries.

5. Dynamic Headers that Look Great at Any Size

Your new responsive real estate website should have a header graphic that adjusts to the size of the device its on automatically. With smaller devices, you want to make sure that the most important parts of the page are still prominent when the rest of the page is reduced. No matter what kind of device you are on, make sure your branding looks great! Whether its being looked at on a desktop, a laptop or a smartphone, your brand and logo should still be up front and making its permanent mark in everyone's subconscious database.

6. Navigation that is Easy to Find, Easy to Use

No matter what kind of device your site is being viewed on, easy navigation is vital! Responsive designs must follow the same guidelines. Your design must provide access to the most visited areas of your website and at the same time keep the emphasis on your content.

7. Don't Sacrifice Function for Form

We've outlined how important the visual aspect of your site on any device is important for today's conditioned consumer, but let's not forget how important keeping the desktop functionality is. A responsive site should still allow easy registration so that your prospects can save their specific searches and favorite listings, with the ability to come back later and jump back in the same spot. This is how you become the invaluable homes for sale resource.

8. Content is Still King More Than Ever

Part of your Unique Selling Proposition that makes you special has to be your intimate knowledge of what makes your area tick. This just can't be replaced with links to local websites where they have crime stats and poverty rates, etc., which don't give your users a warm fuzzy feeling. Your "voice" is what makes you stand out, and it is what Google is also looking for. You want to ensure that your responsive website makes your Blog posts look great and are prominently displayed. And the more your prospects get to know, like and trust you, the person, the easier it will be for them to make those "Come List Me" phone calls.

9. Capturing Leads

With almost 50% of the public doing their real estate searches on a smartphone, you need to make sure that capturing those leads is as easy as on a desktop or laptop. And the easier that your forms, drop-down menus and buttons are to work with, the less likely the user will leave before sending you their contact information.

Don't be Cheap with Your IDX

A quick IDX history: Back in the 20th Century, before the Internet was a dominant force, MLS listings were printed up in big books and distributed by hand. Often the information would be obsolete the moment it was printed before ever reaching the agent.

In the 80s and 90s, many MLS boards started adopting a computer based system that agents could login to via modem and download to their Commodore-like computer system running MS-DOS with a big lunky monochrome monitor on top. Definitely better and more up-to-date than the previous printed version.

Back in these pre-Millennium days, your MLS was run as a non-profit entity to service your needs. You "owned" your listing and your MLS was a benevolent service organization that never intended to make a profit off of you.

Fast forward to 1999. After five years of having to login to a super slow dial-up modem to view the internet, a new normal swept across the country making the Internet more usable for everyone. This was the widespread roll-out of the cable-modem which instantly drove the dial-up modem into the dust. Cable Internet access allowed for easy and quick viewing of anything on the World Wide Web, including all things real estate.

Also in 1999 was the roll-out of a new paradigm called I.D.X., which stands for "Internet Data Exchange." IDX was created to share a sub-set of the MLS data online so that Brokers and Agents could now display this information on their websites for clients to research themselves instead of having to be the constant go-between for clients looking for the right property.

Since searching for home listings became a hot commodity, suddenly non-profit MLS boards found themselves making side deals with Yahoo, MSN, and a large number of other websites who began posting home listings.

To help even the playing field, 3rd Party IDX Providers started popping up to handle the raw data and turn it into a graphically appealing interface for real estate agents to put on their own websites that prospective home buyers could easily use.

Even if the MLS had a "free" IDX portal to search the MLS, it did not allow for branding the pages for the Agent, and usually required that the user click away from the agent site to the MLS provider's site, thus cutting short the "time on site" that the search engines would track how popular your site was.

Even if your MLS offers a free or cut-rate cheap solution for IDX, in most cases this solution will not help your website get more search engine traction, which is why it is so cheap or free with your membership.

There is a reason that 3rd Party IDX Providers exist and why they cost more. It is because they deliver far more value than the freebie IDX searches that are really only meant for starter agents to use.

Just the ability to offer advanced virtual mapping for any community on any page you wish is worth that alone if not just for the "stickiness" it adds to your website keeping users on your site longer.

The difference in cost between a good effective IDX and a lackluster ineffective IDX is less than $50-60 per month on average. Since your "office" where everyone is going to see you and judge you is online, why would you sacrifice giving your prospects the best just to save a miniscule amount as that? There are some places where it just doesn't pay to be cheap, and IDX is definitely one of them.

GET WITH IT!

Don't be that Realtor with the old school site. Be mighty! Show them you have arrived and are a force to be reckoned with. The public knows when they see something that looks just like the same-old same-old they've been looking at for years from every other generic agent.

You *can* have it all... Social... Local... Mobile. And with a modern look as well that makes you appear to be plugged in and not stale, and pre-recession.

BRETT MILLER • CHERI ALGUIRE • ERIC LOFHOLM

The Easy Way To Blog And The
Smart Way To Post To Social Media

What is Blogging?

Why does the word "blogging" make a lot of people shutter like you've asked them to write a term paper or college dissertation?

Though Blogging has been around in one fashion or another since 1983, decades before the term "Internet" was anything the general public had ever heard of.

Blog is the merging of the word "Web" and "Log" - a way for people to record their thoughts on the Internet. Remember on Star Trek when Captain Kirk would enter his verbal "Captain's Log" via the Enterprise's computer? It's exactly the same only much different, but mostly the same.

A "log" is a snapshot in time for you to reflect on something you wish to talk about, and it is in a chronological format so your newest one is at the top. Each "post" is its own web page, and when incorporated into a blog has a connecting thread that makes it easy to browse from beginning to end, unlike disconnected web pages.

Was a blog post meant to be long and boring? Certainly not. And since you decided to be a Realtor instead of the next Ernest Hemingway, we can understand your reticence at having to sit and compose something that even YOU would not read.

It's important because it works! If there's one thing that I continue to repeat to my real estate clients over and over and over, it is that blogging is one of the most effective ways to attract prospects to your real estate website, and you need to be doing it at least weekly.

Six Reasons Why All Real Estate Agents should Blog

1. Search Engine Optimization

Blogging helps your Real Estate website achieve a higher ranking on search engines. The key to search engine ranking is information-rich content being added on a consistent basis. Blogging is the ideal format for publishing information on the Internet, and it's really easy to update a blog. It's truly like writing an email only it's to the whole world. It's even as simple as a short Facebook post.

Every Blog post you publish becomes its own web page adding yet another page of content on the web. The more content you have on your Real Estate website, the more you look like an information-rich website to the search engines looking to "recommend" sites for whatever search term is being used.

2. Credibility

A blog helps to brand you as an expert in local knowledge and in real estate. Blogs are the perfect place to talk about what you know about the area, current happenings, market updates, and real estate news… and it costs you nothing to post them.

When you share your knowledge in a blog, you build the kind of trust and credibility that turns contacts into leads into clients for life. After a while, you will build up a huge inventory of postings, which will be impressive, especially to the Generation X and Y homebuyers that are the future of your business.

3. Relationship Building

Blogs put a personal face on your real estate business. The personal nature of blogs makes them a powerful tool for building relationships with your clients and potential clients. There's a lot of competition online in the real estate space, and a blog is one of the best ways to separate you from the competition. Staying in front of these potential future clients is critical in staying in their hearts and minds when they are finally ready to buy or sell a home. Blogging helps you build the quality of relationships that can turn leads into clients for life. If you don't have a blog, make launching your own blog one of your top priorities.

4. Feedback

Your blog makes instant feedback possible. A blog is an ideal format for getting feedback from clients. Visitors can respond to your comments and link to your blog posts from their own websites, blogs and social media. Hot topics can create a thread that engages dozens – or hundreds of readers to post their replies. The replies will tell you a lot about what your market is thinking and wanting.

5. Up-to-date Information

Blogs put information that is new and that helps you in a couple ways. First, it will give your clients and potential clients reason to come back to your site again and again.

Also, the "spiders" that Google uses to regularly "crawl" your site to see if there's anything new will reward you for the fresh and frequently updated content by giving you higher Search Engine rankings.

Every time Google comes back to see "how you're doing" and discovers that you and your site aren't going to roll over and play dead after putting up your initial 8 page website, they will take note and give you an advantage over the other complacent website owners. Google is drawn to new content as a cat is drawn to catnip. Give Google all the catnip you can and reap the benefits!

6. Blogging Leverages Your Time

Not only can you speak to many people instead of just one with a blog post, you can now have that post be sent to many different groups of people simultaneously using different methods that all work from one click of your submit button.

Why More Realtors Post to Facebook Instead of their own Blog

If you have any original content or photos to share online, they should always be posted to your own website first instead of bypassing your website to post directly into your Facebook and Twitter accounts.

Even though an agent will get no personal SEO by posting content directly to their social profiles, most agents still do this even though this same content could be helping their own website and giving them higher placement.

Many real estate agents are not sure about what to post to their blogs and often their blogs have less than 2 posts per month instead of the recommended 3-5 posts per week. Yet they have no problem posting images and whimsical content to their Facebook page. So why is that?

We think the issue is that there is a perception that your blog needs to be a place where only well-written articles and long term-paper type works of literature are written.

In other words:

>> Facebook = Easy
>> Blog = Difficult

This is not a good perception because it keeps Agents like you from adding content to your own Blog which then keeps you from being recognized as a consistent content provider by Google and the other search engines. Since content creation is now their most important criteria for giving good placement on their search engine, I would say this is an important point to understand.

Question: What if posting to your Blog was easy? And what if your Blog would automatically then broadcast that post to your Facebook and Twitter? You'd be killing two birds with one stone. And you'd be doing the right thing to make your website more attractive to Mr. Google.

Still, it would have to be easy, right?

So what would you post? The truth is, what your website needs is a big dose of "local" from you. Post lots of photos of EVERYTHING around town, and the adjacent communities. And not all at once… just one-at-a-time AS you see the opportunity right from your smartphone. Think about how you can drip-drip-drip this great content on a consistent basis instead of dumping it all at once like out of a bucket.

And those other posts should be posted to your website and THEN automatically re-posted to your Facebook and Twitter accounts. (We call this "broadcasting.")

Facebook's War on Boring

Do you realize that if nobody ever "Likes" or Shares" your Facebook posts that you will simply stop appearing on their Facebook News Feed? That's because Facebook doesn't want you to be bored and stop using their service. If people never respond to your posts, never like them, never share them, never comment to them, then it must be because you are BORING.

That's why posting photos and videos is so important!

Imagine having your own Secret Virtual Blogging Assistant, a V.A. that you don't pay. This is a system where you just email your photo to your secret email address along with a good subject line and a caption underneath. And make sure you always ask people to "Like" or "Share" your photo if they like it.

Or use an easy App we will direct you to put on your smartphone so that you can use it just like you would use the Facebook app, and then easily post those photos and captions to your own website which then will automatically post the same content to your Facebook and Twitter profiles.

The Easy Way to Blog with Your Secret Virtual Blogging Assistant

Imagine you are driving down one of your favorite neighborhoods in the springtime at the exact moment when flowers are bursting in front of the town square.

You pull out your smartphone and capture the scene perfectly on your phone's camera. Then, instead of sharing the photo via your Facebook app, you instead open another app that connects to your website, you then attach the photo, create a short subject line for your email, then write a quick sentence or two describing what you saw, and ending with "Please like or share this."

Now imagine clicking the "submit" button on your app and the following 5 things happen automatically:

1. The post with photo publishes to your website's Blog

2. The same post is also displayed on your Home Page in the featured posts with a thumbnail of the photo.

3. The post is automatically "broadcast" to your Facebook business page (and personal page if you wish).

4. The post is automatically "broadcast" to your Twitter profile.

5. On Friday morning, that post along with every other post you've added to your site in the past week is automatically added to an e-newsletter that is sent out to your entire database of clients along with links to view the latest listings for sale in your market.

All of these important mediums for you to communicate with, all done with one simple Facebook-like operation. And you didn't have to do them in 5 steps from your computer. They were all done while you were in the moment from the convenience of your personal Mobile device. Don't you think this is something you could do? Yes, you could!

If you don't have a Secret Virtual Blogging Assistant now with your current website, get one!

Become the Local Lifestyle Ambassador

This idea is not about posting real estate information even. It is about you being "in the moment" and sharing what you like best about the area you live in. We call that being a "Lifestyle Ambassador." The more you post positive images and feelings about your area and your market online, the more likes, comments and good feelings you will collect in return. You will be thought of as the positive person who makes them feel good and not the cranky person complaining about politics or other divisive subjects.

The 80/20 Rule

This brings us to the 80/20 Rule of posting. 80% of your posts should not be business or real estate oriented. That's 5 out of 6 posts that should be fun and positive local lifestyle oriented postings all with a beautiful picture that will catch their attention and make them agree to Like or Share the post.

Every Thursday, make it a habit to post whatever events are happening around your area. Include the new movies opening. Talk about the local high school play or musical or sporting events. Your market is interested in this content even if they are not currently thinking about real estate. Give them a reason to not ignore your posts and emails.

Then 20% (that's 1 out of 5) should be real estate oriented. Just Listeds, Just Solds, Just Reduceds, Market Conditions, Hot Buys. When mixed in with the other 80% of non-real estate oriented content, there is a better chance of these posts being seen and read, and that you will not be perceived as being just a real estate robot with no soul.

When you don't bore people, they will Like and Share you more

Remember, the more someone engages with your post online, the higher the probability will be that they will see your business and real estate oriented posts for the other 20%. That's why it's so important to capture their hearts first and foremost, so that when their minds are finally focused on real estate, you will be top of mind and the Realtor they will want to talk to.

Make people you don't know feel like they do know you.

As the adage goes, people want to do business with those they know, like and trust. Just like you may feel you know someone from reality TV or the local news anchors more than you know your own neighbors, the same will happen when you have a consistent "presence" in their lives via your posts which will be delivered on their social media, in their email, and on your website.

BRETT MILLER • CHERI ALGUIRE • ERIC LOFHOLM

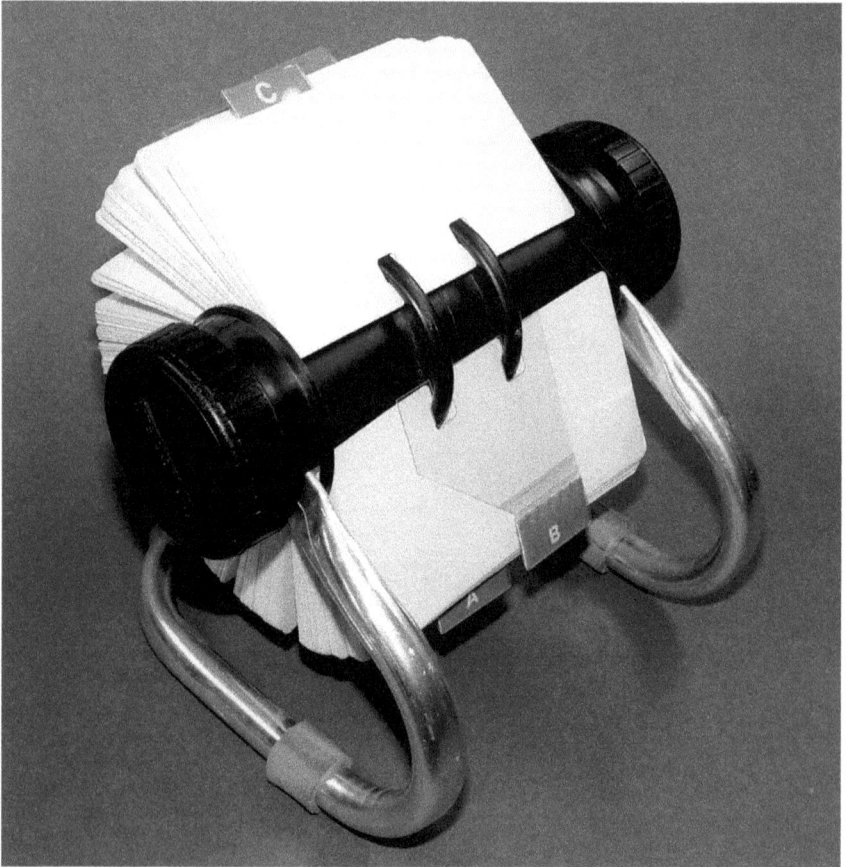

Your List:
Your Most Valuable Asset

The Money is in the List:
Creating and Organizing Your Prospect List

If you've been listening at all to the plethora of marketing experts everywhere the last few years, overwhelmingly the main point they make is that you must "build your list." This is your contact list of people you know, people you've met, and people you've already done business with. In the 20th Century, this meant having a full "Rolodex."

If you saw the final episode of "Mad Men" you would have seen the savvy former secretary Joan Harris starting a money-making business quickly because of the impressive number of contacts in her Rolodex (her list). Joan built her list over 10 years. You probably have as well, even if it is not organized yet into a recognizable form.

Creating a targeted real estate prospect list will need extra work. Getting a drilled-down list that will meet your ideal prospect profile will need a little more work. This will be time well spent and it will pay dividends for years to come.

How to Create your Ideal Real Estate Prospect list

You will need to learn how to create, organize and manage your list with whichever CRM (Customer Relationship Management) system you choose to use. In effect, your CRM is the software program that holds your contact database that you will use to communicate to your list.

Once you get your Contacts sorted out and imported, using your website as the vessel, you can automatically stay in touch with your list on a consistent basis and keep yourself top-of-mind as their "Realtor of Choice."

Cleaning Up Your Contact List

OK, geeks. This section is for you! Many Agents use many different types of online databases from different companies, including your email contact list, your MLS, different lead aggregators, and any system you've used through the years that collects contact information for you to use. It would not be unusual to have four or more of these type of lists out there with none of them being combined into one super-list… until now.

Learn how to "export" your contacts into CSV (Comma Separated Values) files. The goal will be then to import all of the separate CSV files into a single master Excel spreadsheet document.

Once you've imported each set of contacts, add a column called "Source" and enter where that set of contacts came from for future reference.

If you notice that on some contacts that the Name is not separated into First Name and Last Name, you will want to do this now. Then move the Last Name column into first position on the left side as Column A, with First Name next to it as Column B, and Email Address as Column C.

After all of your separate CSV files are imported in and edited as described above, its now time to "Sort" the entire document by Last Name (primary) and First Name (secondary). The resulting list will make it very easy to spot the duplicates and to make a master contact with all the needed info and to delete the unneeded duplicate.

NOTE: If you see a duplicate with different email addresses, you will want to select the most likely email. A lot of old contacts may show an AOL, Yahoo or EarthLink address which most people have moved on from a long time ago. Many people may still be using these older systems, but in case of a duplicate, consider this when making your pick for which to keep.

Now, go through and delete people you do not want to be in contact with, like spammers, newsletters, and people who you really are not in personal contact with.

OK, by this point your list should be looking pretty good to use as an email database. Quickly go down the spreadsheet checking to see if there are any empty email cells in the spreadsheet. If there are, you or your admin will need to do some investigation work to see if you can find the missing email addresses online by searching Google, Facebook, their company website, etc. If you can't locate the email address, consider making a quick phone call if you know the person and simply asking for it.

If at the end, you can not find that person's email, you should either delete their record or move it to another spreadsheet for contacts that are missing email addresses.

By now, your list should really be in ship-shape. Now lets insert some great extra functionality. Add 2 columns to help you CATEGORIZE and SUBCATEGORIZE all your contacts:

CATEGORIES:

> Contacts
> Prospects
> Clients
> Referral Partners

CONTACTS

Your goal with this category: This category is for ALL your contacts. Everybody is a contact. You can sub-categorize your "Contacts" like this:

> Contacts: Sphere
> Contacts: Family
> Contacts: BNI/Chamber (or any professional or charity groups)
> Contacts: Vendors
> Contacts: Other Realtors
> Contacts: Personal
> Contacts: General

PROSPECTS

Your goal with this category: To move people from "Contacts" to "Prospects"

> Prospects: Buyers
> Prospects: First-Time Buyers
> Prospects: Sellers
> Prospects: Farm
> Prospects: Military

CLIENTS

Your goal with this category: To move people from "Prospects" to "Clients". You would enter the YEAR you had them as a client (or you could separate it in a more intuitive way to you.).

> Clients: 2016
> Clients: 2015
> Clients: 2014 (separate by year if you choose)

REFERRAL PARTNERS

Your goal with this category: To turn "Clients" into "Raving Fans" who will then send you Referrals, thus becoming "Referral Partners"

Once your Excel Spreadsheet is all completed, we can then import the database into Mailchimp or another CRM of your choice.

NOTE: THIS IS A VERY IMPORTANT TASK THAT WILL MAKE YOU MONEY.

Gather Home Addresses, Birthdays, and Home Anniversaries (when someone closed their house you sold them). Once you have all of this, we will show you how to use a Relationship Marketing System we have already set up for you so that everyone you want to stay in contact with will keep you "top of mind."

What is the best way to get people to subscribe to your list?

Along with people you will be adding from your Gmail list and other contacts you've collected from other sources, going forward our goal is to get new people to sign up on your "list."

To accomplish this, we recommend that you offer some kind of "ethical bribe" – either a "Special Report" that someone in your market would find so compelling that they will enter their name and email address (perhaps a title like "7 Crucial Things You Must Know Before Listing Your Home in <<your area>>") or a service like signing up to get new home listings in their area as soon as they go on the market. Perhaps you've written a book and it is already on Amazon.com and you are offering a PDF of your book at no charge.

Communicating with your List

What will you send these people who are signed up?

With any modern website, you should have 3 easy ways of adding content to your website:

1) Regular Blogging using the WordPress "Post" system

2) Sending email to your own website using your Secret Virtual Blogging Assistant Email Address

3) Using an App on your smartphone like you would Facebook on your phone to send Photos to your Blog.

In addition to these "Posts" being automatically Broadcast to your Facebook and Twitter, your website should have a built-in email marketing system to automatically create a weekly digest of all your Blog Posts and email them as an eNewsletter.

That means that if you posted 3 beautiful photos of your area to your blog, a personal note about the summer market, and perhaps an Open House or Just Listed during the week, and a Weekend Events post, all of these would be included in the Weekly Enews that would be sent out automatically on a weekly basis.

This is how you will use your List to create a database that will become the genesis of the automated enewsletter program that will automatically compile your week's worth of Blog posts and send them as a weekly newsletter and keep you top of mind with everyone you know as their Realtor of Choice.

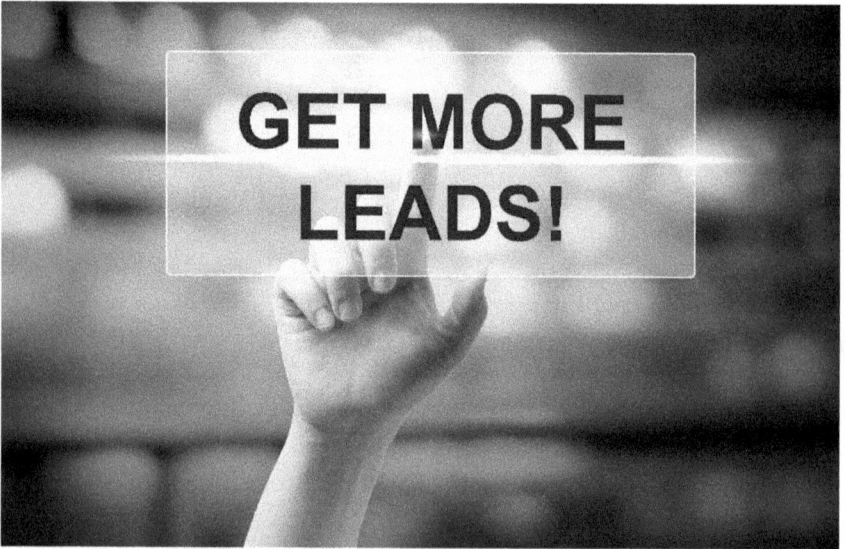

Lead Generation

You have your database all set up. Your past clients, sphere, family and friends are all entered into your CRM. The task took a little time, but now it is done! You have your email marketing set up to go out on a weekly basis. Now what? It is important to continue to do lead generating activities to continue to add to this pipeline. What is most effective?

Lead generating comes in two basic forms, Online and Offline. Some of these activities are free and others will involve fees ranging from minimal to substantial. Let's start out talking a little about Online Lead Generation.

We have already talked about the most important aspect of all of your Lead Generation, the cornerstone of all of your Online and Offline Marketing, your Online 'Storefront,' your website.

Your website is the most important way for you to collect online leads. Your contact form should funnel your leads into your database and an auto responder should start as well as you need to be in contact with these new leads.

It is important to have some sort of a Lead Magnet on your website. The days where you could say "Sign up for my eNewsletter" and have that be effective for getting people to put their name and email address into a form and send it to you are long over. However, that Special Report of 'The 9 Reasons Omaha, Nebraska is a Great Place to Raise a Family,' or 'Why Tampa, Florida is a Great Place to Buy Real Estate," will get people looking to buy a home in these areas to fill out a form and give you their contact information, all because of a great lead magnet.

Other ideas for a great lead magnet include 'Lists' such as "The Top 10 Waterfront Properties under $250,000" or "5 Open Houses This Weekend You Don't want to Miss!"

You can use the same Lead Magnets on Social Media. Just remember to always have the lead click back to your website, the Cornerstone of your Marketing, to fill out the contact form. The other things you have on your website that we mentioned earlier such as the Pop-up Chat Feature and Sticky Maps, will give you more opportunities to capture the lead than just using Social Media avenues alone.

You can also use your Personal Lead Websites, Lead Pages, or Landing Pages. What do I mean by that? These are one page websites that do not necessarily have your personal branding and navigation all over them like your personal website.

On the Internet, what exactly is a "Landing" Page?

Simply put, a "Landing" page is a standalone webpage that has a specific intention to offer a product or service and to collect the needed information from the interested party so that you the Agent get their information and they get whatever was offered.

Often, a unique domain name is purchased just for that one page and that URL can be placed in your email signature as well as being an easy-to-remember website address to tell others about verbally.

So, what is needed to create an effective Landing Page? Let me outline the steps below:

1) Branded vs. Non-Branded (Stealth)

A "Branded" site means that your name, logo and image are right there on the page just like on the rest of your website. This is much faster to create than a non-branded site because your website's "theme" (if you are setup on a WordPress website) is already set and just the content needs to be added. In this instance, all of your website's navigation is in place for the visitor to browse through

A non-branded or "Stealth" website means that your name, image and logo may not be on the page at all. Or it can be. Your choice. The main distinction is that no other navigation to the rest of your website is available. A Stealth webpage usually takes a little longer to program because of the custom nature of it.

2) Headline

The Headline is the big big line of bold text centered at the top of the web page. It should be very well written with keywords in it so that the search engines will note the "Headline" tag on it and give importance to those words. So you need to know what you want the Headline for each of your Landing pages to be.

3) URL/Website Address

The URL (website address) can be almost identical to Headline (same words). You can "goose" (enhance) the URL by adding the words to add helpful geographic SEO. An example would be if the Headline was "How much do homes in your neighborhood cost?" – so your URL with geographic words in it might be /how-much-do-homes-in-your-flagstaff-az-neighborhood-cost/ – Note how we added in "flagstaff-az" into the URL to make it more findable for anyone searching in the Flagstaff AZ area.

4) Content: Text

What is the specific text you want to be on the Landing Page? Think of this as an informational flyer you are handing out. Write out all the text in a Word document so that you can bold and italicize the text where you want it, then email this document to your webmaster.

5) Content: Photos

Photos must have authorization to use. Many uninformed people think every image on the Internet is "free" to use and then they pull copyrighted photos from the web. We know of many true stories of clients who have done this and received a bill for over $2,000 for unauthorized use from the photographer or stock photo service's attorney. Don't let this happen to you!

There are many inexpensive stock photo services where images can be anywhere from $1 to $5 each for a low resolution photo that will be perfectly good for web page use, as opposed to print use which requires a file four times as large.

6) Video

Video is the #1 most powerful tool you can use on your website. Especially if you have uploaded it to YouTube and have entered the transcription of the text into the YouTube Video Description area. (As well as a link to the page.) Once you have your video on YouTube, send the "Embed Code" to your webmaster so that they can place your video on your page.

7) Opt-in Form

The most important reason for your Landing Page is to collect the contact information from the person visiting it. Other than First Name, Last Name and Email address, what other information do you need? (TIP: Don't ask for any more than you need or the person filling out the form may balk and not complete the process.)

Where do you want the form data to be emailed to? Just you? To you and an administrator?

Do you want something to be emailed to the person who fills it out? If so, is it ready to be attached to an email to send? Or do you want a link to that document in an auto-responder email?

8) Thank You Page

On the "Thank You" page after somebody has successfully completed the form, you have an amazing opportunity to "continue the conversation" once somebody has made the decision to opt-in by filling in the blanks and hitting the submit button.

Do you want to have a link to download a report?

Do you want another marketing message with another video?

Don't squander the opportunity to continue the conversation!

When you ask to have a Landing Page created for you, make sure you have already collected the information for the 8 points listed above, and you will be able to have your Landing Page created in record time.

Paid Ads

We couldn't talk about Online Lead Generating without talking about Paid Ads. You can pay for Online Ads with Google and Social Media like Facebook. A Lead Magnet or a Landing Page website are great ways to drive leads from searches to your website or landing page. When doing pay-per-click or Facebook Ads, make sure you are watching your budget and analyzing your results closely. You will have access to great reporting and it is important to monitor these numbers as well as set a budget and stick to it! You can also hire out the Pay-Per-Click and Facebook advertising.

There are also online lead sites such as ExpiredRealEstateLeads.com, FSBORealEstateLeads.com, Tiger Leads and Bold Leads as well as Zillow, Trulia and so many others. Many of these lead companies will sell you leads based on the zip code you purchase, or will offer you and many other agents the same leads, making it crucial that you are the one that is following up the fastest and best.

With any of these online marketing avenues, make sure you have your budget set, make sure you are collecting these leads into your database so you can follow up past the initial contact, and make sure you have your scripts set so you are not winging it. We will talk more of that in the next chapter. If you wing it, you will get wing it results.

While Online Leads may be a major focus, don't rule out Offline activities. The most obvious offline activity would be a local networking group such as BNI, LeTip, or Chamber of Commerce meetings. But don't forget about the people you meet through PTA, your Golf Lessons, or weekly Bunko Group. You are meeting people all of the time. Building relationships with these people and offering value will help you continue to build your list.

Later in this book we will also talk about ways you can continue to build relationships, move people through the pipeline and develop a platform where you are known as the local expert!

Why Learning Sales Scripting
Is So Valuable

Why is knowing sales scripting so valuable? In my experience, scripting is the best way to help you overcome some of the biggest frustrations in real estate sales. It is also the best way to generate revenue consistently. Sales scripting can help you:

- Overcome anxiety stemming from not knowing what to say during a sales presentation

- Build confidence in your ability to speak, close, and handle objections effectively

- Know what to say in any sales situation, whether speaking one-on-one, from the front of the room, over the phone, or over a webinar

- Ensure that your sales presentations always follow a persuasive sequence steering a clear path to a strong close

- Avoid losing sales by delivering a close prematurely before you've laid a foundation with rapport, probing questions, and benefits

- Build trust and rapport quickly and easily

- Hone your probing questions to identify what your prospect really wants and what's going to make them want to buy

- Present your benefits using powerful words that arouse your prospect's desires

- Close smoothly and naturally without anxiety

- Handle objections with the confidence that comes from being prepared and knowing exactly what to say

- Know how to follow up to turn one sales opportunity into multiple opportunities

- Generate referrals on a regular basis

- Get consistent, predictable sales results from following the same successful script over and over

Why You Should Embrace Scripting

A first step towards getting past fear of sounding scripted is appreciating the value of scripting. Tens of thousands of real estate agents have used sales scripting to increase the number of transactions they complete each you. In my sales career over the past two decades, I've used scripting to generate nearly $500 million revenue for my clients.

Why do scripts work? Simple: human beings respond in predictable ways. Let me give you an example. If you do what a millionaire does, you'll get what a millionaire has. If you invest your money where millionaires currently have their money invested, what will you become? If you were with me here today, you would say, "A millionaire."

Now, I've asked that question to literally thousands of people, and every person — every person — gives the same answer: a millionaire.

"Prediction is a form of power" — Dr. Moine

In your presentation, wouldn't you like to know what your prospects are going to say before they say it? Well, that is the power of sales scripting.

Because audience reactions to scripts are predictable, you can borrow other people's scripts. I didn't make up from scratch the script I just shared with you about the millionaire. I borrowed it from someone else. You can do the same: borrow other people's scripts.

If you're still not sure about the power of scripting, listen to what Michael Gerber, one of the world's leading experts on teaching business owners how to raise their level of success and the man behind the book The E-Myth, has to say about scripting. This is a direct quote from the book:

Things need to be sold and it's usually people who have to sell them. Everyone in business has heard of the old song 80 percent of our sales are produced by 20 percent of our people. Unfortunately few seem to know what the 20 percent are doing that the eighty percent aren't.

The 20 percent use a system, unlike the other 80 percent!

Let's take this a step farther. Sales scripting is part of your selling system, a fully orchestrated interaction between you and your customer. A selling system follows five primary steps:

• Step 1: Identification of the specific benchmarks or consumer decision points in your selling process.

• Step 2: The literal scripting of the words that will get you to each consumer decision point successfully. (Yes, written down, like the script for a play.)

• Step 3: The creation of various materials to be used with each script.

• Step 4: The memorization of each benchmarked script.

• Step 5: The delivery of each script by your sales representatives in identical fashion.

If you put a sales system involving scripting to work in your company, you will see amazing results regardless of what kind of business you're in.
– Michel Gerber

You're Already Using a Script, But Is It a Good Script?

At this point you might be saying, "Okay, Eric, I see how scripting can make me more money, but that doesn't really address my concern about sounding artificial. Won't scripting make me sound less natural and hurt my sales delivery?"

Here's the answer to that I tell audiences:

The reality is, whether you think you're using scripts or not, you are using scripts.

Now you might be saying to yourself right now, "Eric, you don't know what you're talking about. I don't use sales scripts." Yes, you do, and I will share with you why shortly. For now, here's an interesting question: Why do people resist scripting? Most people respond by saying they don't want to sound canned, rehearsed, inauthentic, robotic, they don't feel that scripts are flexible, and so on. If that were my view of what scripting is, then I wouldn't want to use scripts either.

However, what if that's not what scripting is? What if scripting is something totally different? What if scripting made you more powerful, more persuasive, and helped you and your client at the same time? Would you want to learn more about it? Its power? How it can transform you into a persuasion master? If this speaks to you, then you are reading the right material, at the right time.

If scripting isn't canned, or rehearsed, or inauthentic, or robotic, or inflexible, what is it? Here is Dr. Moine's reply:

A script is a series of words in sequence that have meaning.

In other words, a script is the opposite of a random string of words. This is why I say that in reality, we all use sales scripts. You're either using a script or you're speaking in random gibberish.

Of course, you don't speak in gibberish. Let me give you an example. Suppose that I asked you to deliver a presentation today, one that you've never delivered before. You would probably get the details from me, then deliver the best presentation possible. The second time you delivered this presentation, you would repeat much of what you said the first time. The third time you delivered this presentation, a lot of what you said the first and second times you'd say again. In other words, you would have effectively drifted into a script. People think, "Oh, I don't use scripts because I don't want to be scripted!" In reality, however, you are scripted; it's just that you drifted into a script.

If you accept the fact that you use scripts, the key question then becomes this: how effective are your scripts? You have two choices. You can either continue to wing it, creating your scripts by drifting into them. Or, you can prepare powerful, persuasive scripts that will make you more confident, more consistent, and add more value to your clients, all of which will bring you more business day after day, presentation after presentation, for the rest of your career.

Consider this example: When a world leader like the President or the Pope or a business leader addressing a group of investors makes a speech, do you think that he makes up that speech as he goes along? Or do you think he's using a prepared script? You see, when everything counts; people use a prepared script.

Or imagine that you were the owner of an organization that has fifty salespeople. Would you want them using persuasive scripts, or would you want them making up their presentations on the fly, so to speak? Of course you would want them using persuasive scripts.

Scripts absolutely are flexible. They are powerful. They are prepared. They are persuasive. Simply put, sales scripting is the most powerful way for you to improve your presentation results. Wow, pretty important, right? Let me repeat that . . . seven times:

Sales scripting is the most powerful way for you to improve your presentation results!

Sales scripting is the most powerful way for you to improve your presentation results!

Sales scripting is the most powerful way for you to improve your presentation results!

Sales scripting is the most powerful way for you to improve your presentation results!

Sales scripting is the most powerful way for you to improve your presentation results!

Sales scripting is the most powerful way for you to improve your presentation results!

Sales scripting is the most powerful way for you to improve your presentation results!

Here are some great tips to really improve your real estate scripts:

Create an outline of your presentation so you the sequence you want to cover with the prospect. You can do this for a buyer or seller presentation. You can always deviate from the outline if your intuition is guiding you to. By creating an outline you will be more confident prior to meeting with the prospect.

Use success stories of people you have helped with their real estate. When you tell stories it helps the prospect get connected to how you can help them. If you are doing a listing presentation you might share a story of another home that you sold where your marketing created so many potential buyers that the price when $10,000 over listing price. You can also share stories of how quickly you have sold properties or how effectively you negotiated for your client. Tell the same stories over and over again.

Develop a close to a point where you practically know it word-for-word. At the end of a buyer presentation you can say the some thing to each prospect. When you do this it builds your confidence. This is true because the more you say the same thing the more you internalize it. When you project certainty in the close it increases the likelihood the prospect buys from you.

Develop a list of probing questions to identify what is most important to your prospect. This is a very simple idea but it really works. You can close a listing 80% by asking great probing questions.

How To Have More Repeat And Referral Business:
Be A Master Of Follow-Up

Ever consider the cost of LOST BUSINESS because you did not stay in touch with past clients who forgot about you when they were ready to sell their house and buy a new one? It is crucial for you to have a system that will keep you TOP-OF-MIND with your clients. This one idea will outline how you could KEEP THOUSANDS OF DOLLARS in commissions instead of letting them slip through your fingers.

Has this ever happened to you? You were in the grocery store and you see a past client across the produce department. She calls out to you. "Oh, I wish I had known you were still around. Since I never heard from you after we closed on our home, I assumed that you had moved away or you were doing something else. I just hired another Realtor to list my home. We are expecting another baby and needed to find a bigger house."

Ouch! How much income did you miss out on in this one scenario? Assuming they sold House 1 for $200,000, the Gross Closed Commissions would be around $6,00 and assuming you are on a 70/30 spilt, you would net about $4,200.

Let's say they bought House 2 for $375,000. Gross Closed Commissions on this house would be around $11,250 with a net to you of $7,875. From just this scenario you would have made over $12,000. This doesn't include future buys or sells or referrals lost. If she had several friends she also referred to this other agent, you may have lost considerably more.

Here are a few ALARMING STATISTICS. The number one reason a client does not come back and use you again is because they forgot about you. 95% of your happy clients will purchase from a competitor on an impulse. For each month that you don't communicate with your clients, you lose 10% of your influence.

So what can you do to keep this unfortunate and costly series of events from happening to you?

Most real estate agents think that the journey is over as soon as they get the deal done. However, if you truly want to succeed in the industry, then it might be a good move to take note of Billy's Birthday, Dad's Fishing Tournament and Mom's Social Event of the Season. The key is Relationship Marketing.

What is Relationship Marketing? Relationship Marketing is a relationship management strategy designed to encourage strong, lasting connections to your brand. The goal is to turn prospects into customers that generate repeat sales and encourage word-of-mouth promotion (referrals).

Relationship Marketing must follow the 80/20 Rule. Reach out in the spirit of building relationships first, (80% of the time: for things like thank yous, birthdays, holidays,) and marketing second (20% of the time).

The Real Estate Agent who gets the ideas in this chapter can transform their business to one that focuses on building by it with repeat clients and referrals. These referrals are already interested in buying or selling. Imagine how much time and resources are saved through this approach. Now you won't need to run after potential clients. Instead, prospects are now coming to you.

5 Keys to Creating a Successful Referral Marketing Business

1. Ability to create relationships with a large network of people that know what you do through Friendship, Celebration and Service.

Relationships just don't come out of thin air. As a Realtor, you must actually break that barrier that's preventing you from becoming a friend.

This involves Recognizing, Listening and Acting on your Promptings – Be "that" person who celebrates others. One good way to do this is through Listening to Life with Relationship Marketing Ears.

(Psssst! We are in the People Business, not the Houses Business.)

Do you believe that? Now it is true that you do have to have a working knowledge of home basics. If you don't know what a water heater looks, like or the difference between a Rambler and a Split, you may have some challenges being in this industry. However, having a background in structural engineering won't help you either, unless you have clients to work with.

I am sure you have heard the old saying "They don't know how much you know, until they know how much you care." But how do you show people how much you care?

Well let me ask you this? Are you on Facebook? Do you post information on your new listing or latest price reduction? Probably. And that is fine. But, is that the ONLY thing you post? If it is, you probably get past clients and friends tuning you out. You also have to connect with them on a personal level. As human beings we are craving connection with each other.

So how are you staying connected? Let me know what is working for you.

You may want to try connecting on Facebook, or sending a personal email, or handwritten note. A great way a lot of my coaching clients are sending personal notes is with www.CardsForRealEstate.com

Here are just a few easy, inexpensive ways you can let your sphere and past clients know you care and to keep your name top of mind when they here of someone looking to buy or sell:

- Birthday Cards

- Anniversary of their house sale cards

- Thank you cards

- Let's do lunch cards

- Get well cards

- New baby cards

- Congratulation cards

Spending just a few minutes each day connecting with your sphere and past clients can help lift someone's spirits, remind them of who you are and the great job you did for them, and help them to remember you when others are asking them if they know a good real estate agent.

Because people DO want to know how much you care!

One very important point, DO NOT MIX THESE WITH MARKETING! Never include you business card or add "P.S. I appreciate your referrals." You will be ten times more effective if you celebrate people just to celebrate people. It is okay to have branding on the back of the card, but make the front and inside about the receiver of the card, not about you.

2. Ability to consistently follow up and stay top of mind with your clients and prospects.

67% of business today is driven by personal referral and word-of-mouth. What are you doing to maintain customer loyalty (repeat business)?

There are a lot of Realtors out there who are also trying to make a name for themselves. So how do you get clients to remember you as their favorite Realtor? On the first point, I talked about getting recognized. Now, we're going to focus our efforts on maintaining relationships with our clients through easy and affordable follow-ups.

Make sure to consistently follow up with them through balanced efforts. Otherwise, instead of being the coolest friend ever, you'll come off as both annoying and sales-like. Enjoying a 98% referral business takes a bit of effort but it's totally worth it. With CardsForRealEstate.com, you can create groups and send a card you designed to multiple recipients with the click of a button. You could send different holiday cards to different groups; you could send 70 to one group, 100 to another and 300 to a different group, all in just a click of a button?

One thing I would encourage you to do is to identify your TOP referral partners. It's the highest level of contact that you are going to have in your contact manager. Those are the people who you really want to show appreciation and gratitude. It's really easy to do this with CardsForRealEstate.com; we have flowers for Valentines Day; we've got gifts candy, and gift cards. This is a system to automate the way you thank people who are always giving you referrals.

CardsForRealEstate is an Internet-Based Greeting Card/Gifting Relationship Marketing System with a CRM built in. Used consistently, it creates a revolution of kindness and more importantly…a referral business

3. Ability to cost effectively run a long term follow up relationship marketing campaign.

Allow Campaigns to be the heartbeat of your referral business! It's 100% automated, but are still personalized custom referral cards that YOU write. No matter what, make these heartfelt and fun. You shouldn't have to always ask for referral because you should have earned the right to be referred.

What we recommend to most of our clients is to develop a 7 card campaign such as this.

Thank You. For the first time they sent a referral or for doing business with us.

Birthdays. You may also want to take note of their spouse and children's birthdates. Again, this is easy to use with CardsForRealEstate's contact manager.

Off Holidays. Don't just think Christmas! Try to play with other holidays such as Valentines, St. Patricks, Halloween and Thanksgiving. This will help you stand out from the competition. I mean, how many cards do you receive on Thanksgiving?

Asking for Referrals. Again, keeping up with our principle: 80% relationship, 20% marketing.

Or you can do another campaign that's set up for the following events:

Thank You

Follow Up

Holiday

Birthday with a gift

4th of July

Spring Market

Anniversary

The total cost of the above campaign is as little as $19.26 which already includes cards, gifts and shipping.

4. Ability to automate your follow up and relationship building efforts.

We've already mentioned the advantages of putting our clients into groups, and this is so easy to do with CardsForRealEstate. But another thing we could make use of this automated process is when we're farming out for potential clients. Now again, I want to remind you: it's 80% relationship and just 20% marketing. When I talk about farming cards, I'm referring to cards that you would send to a particular neighborhood where you might be farming as a real estate agent. This might be a great time for you to take photos of your area and just send it with market update stats. CardsForRealEstate also allows you to send postcards to your contacts. That's a great way to use SOC to send more of a marketing message. What I suggest is that you make it a little more personal. Instead of just putting your picture in the front, why not put a photo of their neighborhood sign on it. That would grab their attention a little bit more. Make it personal for their area.

Celebrate things like home anniversaries. CardsForRealEstate makes it so easy to do because there's a field in the contact manager specifically for anniversary reminders. This is a great way to build relationships with first homebuyers. It also has one for birthdays, so try sending Billy a box of brownies, caramels or other gift each year. The next time they'll look for a listing agent, they're not going to look for some stranger, but instead, they'll remember someone who never forgets Billy's birthday.

SALES STATISTICS

- 48% of sales people never follow up with a prospect
- 25% of sales people make a second contact and stop
- 12% of sales people only make three contacts and stop
- Only 10% of sales people make more than three contacts
- 2% of sales are made on the first contact
- 3% of sales are made on the 2nd contact
- 5% of sales are made on the 3rd contact
- 10% of sales are made on the 4th contact
- 80% of sales are made between the 5th -12th contact

Use greeting cards to stand out and to automate your follow up efforts.

5. Ability to separate yourself from all other competitors and marketing messages.

With CardsForRealEstate your relationship with your clients is different and special!

You create Custom Closing Cards that make a difference. You Include Gifts and Gift Cards on your thank you and referral cards.

You celebrate First Time Homebuyers in a special way. You can take personal photos of your new client in their new home and implement them into the cards.

You celebrate Home Anniversaries.

You celebrate Friendships.

You celebrate the people you meet.

You celebrate Life's Special Occasions.

Your cards are sent in a real envelope!

Build your business by becoming a Master in Relationship Marketing! Focus on Client Relationship first and Marketing second. Create strong relationships, celebrate life, and be grateful.

Enjoying a 98% referral business takes a bit of effort but it's totally worth it.

I would encourage you to identify your top referral partners. Starting out that may just mean mom dad and your aunt. Once you have those people identified, you will want to send cards 4-6 times a year to say hello, thank you, or happy holiday. No matter what, make these heartfelt and fun. You shouldn't have to always ask for referrals…you should have earned the right to be referred.

You can also use this system for Farming Cards. Use pictures from your area and stats from your market to create interesting cards. Take personal photos of your area and implement them into the cards. Use screenshots of the market statistics to create a fun educational engaging card.

Celebrate Home Anniversaries may be the number one thing you can do to really stand out to your past clients. Think about it, how many other people, even if they helped them move, remember the anniversary date of when someone moved into a new home? You know this closing date and can use the system to set reminders so you will never forget this important date.

Also make sure you always send Custom Closing Cards that makes a difference. Make it personal with photos of the family and the house. Including a gift is also easy, inexpensive, and convenient. More important is the way it makes your buyers feel, especially for those first time homebuyers.

"I've learned that people will forget what you said, people will forget what you did, but people will never forget how you made them feel." — Maya Angelou

Build your business by becoming a Master in Relationship Marketing!

Focus on Client Relationship first and Marketing second. Create strong relationships, celebrate life, and be grateful.

Become "The" Local Expert
By Writing A Book

Being an author has long been looked at as a way to be perceived as an expert in whatever subject you are writing about. A book is now considered to be the ultimate "business card" for a Real Estate Agent gaining credibility. It is also an immeasurably useful tool for gaining access to local media and getting free public relations.

I am not talking about writing the next prize winning book or being the net John Grisham, but I am talking about writing THE book on why your area is the best place to buy a house, or how to choose a Realtor for selling in your area.

Why write a Book?

When you write a book, it gives you credibility with your clients and prospects. Imagine a prospective buyer is surfing the internet looking through the active listings in an area. When they click on your site, they see that you have written the book on "Buying a Home in Austin." That gives you amazing credibility about your competence as a real estate professional. The more credible you are, the more sales you will make because people will trust you more.

Writing a book also sets you apart from other agents. There are hundreds or thousands of Real Estate Agents in your area. There are many things you do to try to stand out from the crowd. Writing a book is a phenomenal differentiator. Again hiring the Realtor who literally 'wrote the book' on "12 Reasons Why Orange County is a Great Place to Live" is a claim that only one agent can make.

Having a book is the ultimate form of advertising. You could use it to send to Listing Prospects, Expireds, FSBOs and even to the local Chamber of Commerce. A book doesn't look like advertising, but it is! You are able to give away free content and knowledge so that people get to know, like and trust you. After reading your short book, you will have already pre-sold your services.

A book is not usually thrown away even after someone reads it, or even if they don't. A paperback book will sit on a shelf or a coffee table until the day they donate it sell it. The fact that the book is sitting on your clients end table will help you gain referrals as their friends come over and see it. Your fancy brochures and email marketing will never get you the same effect.

What kind of book should a local Agent write?

The obvious answer would be to write about what a great place your market area is and write a positive tone about the different neighborhoods, what makes it a great place to raise a family and/or retire, and talk about each area with great affection. And very important… give easy tips on selecting the right real estate agent to trust with their most valuable asset.

"Who would publish my book?"

The beautiful thing about writing a book in this modern era is that you do not have to have a major publisher accept your book, offer you a contract, and have them set up distribution for thousands of copies to be sent worldwide.

You do not even need to have a single copy printed if you don't want to. It can all be done "digitally" and for free (except for the per unit cost of the actual books).

You simply upload your finished Microsoft Word Document and Art files for the book covers up to Amazon.com with their Kindle Direct Publishing service and you are a published author!

If you want old-fashioned printed books, that is also available and it has truly never been easier. Amazon's Publish-on-Demand company CreateSpace.com has the same easy upload capabilities and they don't charge you a cent until you want the physical copies, which for a 6x9 book with 100 pages or less is under $2.50 each.

How big should a book be?

It could be as little as 50 pages or even less! In fact, less is better these days as so many people as so busy that the idea of having to read through some kind of Tolstoy-esque voluminous 300-500 page opus is not likely to happen. Saying something is a "quick-read" is a big plus for most people who want to get your information fast and be able to apply it to their lives.

Imagine on Amazon that someone is searching for anything with the term "Albuquerque" and your book has the title of "I Love ABQ: A Reference Book on all the Family Friendly Neighborhoods in Albuquerque, New Mexico" with a beautiful image of a southwestern home against a beautiful sky. And it only need sell for 99-cents up to $2.99.

Many people don't realize that Amazon is one of the biggest search engines in the world, and everything on Amazon ranks extremely high in Google for their search terms. Amazon is one of the top 10 websites in the entire world out of over a billion websites, after Google, YouTube, Facebook and Yahoo.

How many other real estate professionals in your area are listed in Amazon as an author and real estate expert? None? Why shouldn't you be the first?

What if "selling" your book was not the goal? What if you had no intention on making money from book sales and being the next J.K. Rowling or James Patterson? What would be the point?

A Book is the Ultimate Calling Card to Leave with Prospects

Imagine this scenario: You are making a listing presentation for a luxury home worth $1.5 million dollars. The seller will probably be interviewing many different agents before selecting their Realtor.

After your interview, you say to the seller "Mr. James, this is an important decision and I understand you'll be speaking with many agents before making your selection. Could I ask you to do just one thing before you decide? I wrote a chapter in this book entitled 'How to find a Realtor you can Trust.' I'm certain it will help you make your decision for whomever you choose." Then you will sign a copy of your book and give it to the homeowner.

What would this do to your competition? Answer: They would be blown out of the water!

Give Away Your Book and Meet More Prospects

An innovative client of ours, Dave Swaim of Toney, Alabama, published 3 different books: Wealthy Home Seller Secrets, How to Sell Hard to Sell Homes, and The North Alabama For Sale by Owner Guide. Did Dave write these to become a wealthy author? Heck no! He wrote these to become a wealthy Realtor.

Dave drives people through direct response marketing online and offline to his DaveSwaimAuthor.com website where he gives the books away for free. The person who orders the book enters their mailing address and a day later, Dave drops the book off himself. "I just happened to be in the neighborhood and thought I drop this off to you in person."

Of course, Dave is a real nice guy and people like him right away, and he usually gets the listing.

Books have a Perceived Value

Remember, your Book that is on Amazon has a price attached to it giving it "perceived value" which makes it a valuable tool to use to exchange someone's name, email address, and even their mailing address in exchange for your book.

If you want a FREE option, you could simply send a link to a downloadable PDF version of your book for anyone who signs up via an auto-responder. Or do as Dave Swaim does and invest in copies of your book to deliver in person.

Once your new contact is in your email marketing system, you can then every week send that person and everyone in your subscription database valuable local information and real estate news that is interesting on a consistent basis.

You could even use a PDF of your book as "bait" in a Facebook ad or other online ads where someone could get a "copy" of the book at no charge if they sign up as a subscriber on your website and opt-in to your email list.

"Sounds great, but how would I write a book?"

Writing a book may seem like a daunting task, but it is not. It is absolutely possible to write a book in month, alongside what you are already doing as a busy Real Estate Agent!

We help our clients through this process and it is easier than it may seem. The first thing you need to do is think about what you want to communicate with your reader. Is it about your area? Your expertise in helping Buyers or Sellers? What would your topic be? This will help us create our title and even our subtitle.

Once you have narrowed down the title we will go through a brainstorming exercising listing the things we want to communicate to our prospects who would be reading the book. Make a list of 15-20 topics you could talk about in detail if a prospect asked you about them. Once you have your list, narrow it down to 12 and put them in order.

These 12 topics will turn into the 12 chapters of your book! We will then do the same thing with each Chapter. We will list 15-20 things about each topic we will talk about, cut that to 12 and put those 12 in order.

You could even dictate your ideas into a recording on your smartphone and have a service like iDictate.com transcribe everything very inexpensively.

Many of us consider ourselves as being more of a "numbers person" than a "words person." Having to fill up pages for our first book seemed like a daunting task. This formula helped us expand our words into sentences, into paragraphs into chapters. The first step is to take the 12 topics in the first chapter and turn them into phrases and then questions. By answering the questions, you write the book.

It does take some time, however, using this process you could have a book written in as little as 40 hours.

There are many great resources for creating a book cover publishing with Amazon is easier than ever. We help our clients navigate through this process even coach them on getting their book on the bestseller list if that is something they are interested in. More than anything, a book will add to your credibility, sales, and launch your "platform."

BRETT MILLER • CHERI ALGUIRE • ERIC LOFHOLM

Developing Your Platform

What is a Platform?

A "platform" is what you earn for yourself by being a known expert in your field. It is the reputation you garner from effectively broadcasting your expertise through a variety of methods over a period of time.

Building your platform is very similar to Branding. Your Brand is how people perceive you, and your Platform is the expertise and substance that other people deem you to be a master of, worthy of being listened to on whatever your subject is.

As a real estate professional, when you have built a "platform" on being a Lifestyle Expert for your area, others will listen to you as an authority figure and give you the credibility you wish to have to be come known and trusted locally as a quality Realtor.

Why is this important? In most markets, there are a lot of real estate agents and it is becoming increasingly difficult to stand out and seen as something other than one of the perceived herd of generic Realtors all competing for the same pool of home buyers and sellers. All of them have the same necessary websites and social profiles, though most are in a quandary on how to use them.

Case Study: Tego and Tracy Venturi

When I think of Agents who have successfully built a platform, I immediately think of The Venturi Team from Albuquerque, New Mexico.

Tracy Venturi was the initial spouse to venture into real estate while her husband held down a company job which had him in the office or on the road 5 days a week. Tracy's goal was to "retire" her husband Tego from his day job and for them to build a successful real estate business.

Once the Venturi's decided to go all-in with Personal Branding and tap into blogging and the new world of social media in the late 2000s, their lead faucet just turned on, and business came in at such a rate that Tracy's dream of having Tego join her in the real estate business came to fruition.

Now, with Tego on board full time to implement their Internet marketing strategies, they watched their website's Google rankings go steadily up until they reached the top in their market, followed soon by them becoming the #1 real estate team for their company in the entire state of New Mexico.

By the early 2010s, e-v-e-r-y-b-o-d-y knew The Venturi Team. And not just from their phenomenal sales achievements, but by the amount of "giving back" to their local fellow Realtors by serving on local boards, advocating for better IDX systems from their MLS, and mentoring other agents.

Albuquerque's Fox Newsradio station KIVA 95.9 FM was impressed enough by the Venturis to offer them a weekly radio show to talk about the local real estate market. They've done so well with their show that the popular announcer Eddy Aragon calls them his "two favorite people in real estate." Through that connection and others, the Venturis have been endorsed by big names in the world of talk radio and even Shark Tank real estate expert Barbara Cochran. To top it off, in 2015, Tego Venturi was named Albuquerque Real Estate Salesperson of the Year to honor him for all he has done for their Realtor community.

The point is that the Venturis now have a huge platform of correctly perceived expertise and success that helps them be well known and respected, and that platform has made their business explode even further. In fact, their team attracted so many quality team members, buyer's agents, home sales specialists, administrative staff, that they outgrew their space in their broker's office and had to buy an old Italian restaurant in Albuquerque that they converted into their real estate team headquarters. The sky's the limit now.

The Venturis didn't know any of this stuff when they started, but they had a vision of where they wanted to go. They could imagine the life they wanted for themselves and their children. Being able to take family trips to exotic locations and swim with the dolphins or visit Italy.

Using a Book to Create Your Platform

As mentioned in the previous chapter, a book that you have written (or ghost-written) can be your ticket to getting interviewed by local radio and TV shows as an authority figure on local real estate trends. You may find yourself being interviewed on local radio about real estate. If you're not too shy, you might be like The Venturis and become the radio voice for real estate in your market.

Would it matter if that show was top rated show on the station or if your book was a million seller? No! What matters is that you would have built yourself a platform and forever going forward will be know as an author in addition to being a real estate expert.

Ways to expand your reach and your platform using your book as leverage:

- Speaking at local events such as Lunch and Learns, First Time Buyer Seminars and Chamber of Commerce Programs.

- Radio interviews

- Webinars

- Podcasts

- Video

- TV

If you know you will be on any broadcast, make sure you get a recording of it. Ask the station in advance, or confirm someone you know has the correct technology to record you, and then set up a reminder for them to ensure they don't forget.

Every single time you are in the media gives you added credibility and should be fully utilized on your website and social media.

What if I'm terrified of speaking in public?

It's true that at the top of the list of things that most frighten people, public speaking rates above even death.

Most of us are not born with the public speaking gene. Like almost anything, it is a learned skill. Luckily, an organization that has been around for years can help you not only get over your fear, but can help you really be good at it.

Toastmasters International was formed in 1924 at a YMCA in Santa Ana, California. In the 90+ years since it began, they have helped over four million people learn to effectively speak in public. Today the organization serves over 332,000 members in 135 countries, through its over 15,400 member clubs.

Local chapters meet at all times of the day and some on weekends. Membership is very inexpensive and they have a proven system to help people just like you learn to speak comfortably and confidently. Toastmasters' groups are informal and supportive and its OK to not be good. Everyone there started just like you.

What happens when I build my platform and its wildly successful beyond my dreams?

This will be a wonderful time when you will be setting up multiple systems and team members to work "in" your business so that you can work "on" your business doing the fun networking things and building your platform even more.

BRETT MILLER • CHERI ALGUIRE • ERIC LOFHOLM

How Do You Do It All?

Time Management is a myth. We can't manage time. All we can do is make better choices about what we do with our time. Time is the great equalizer. We all have exactly the same amount of hours in our day. So why do some real estate agents seem to get so much more done in a day? Let's break this down a little bit.

How is your Busyness Doing?

No, I did not mean "Business" but if you tell me how your "Busyness" is, I bet I can tell how your Business is doing. We too often spend far too many hours attending the busy-work of the business, which leaves us tired and short of our goals.

What is on your to-do list for today? Are these items that will get you closer to your goals, or are they just things that you HAVE to do. I can almost bet that if you are getting up every day and just plowing through a seemingly endless to-do list, that your Business may be "surviving," but you are not "thriving."

An important way to tell if you are doing busy work or not, are ask yourself the following questions:

1. Which goal will doing this activity get me one step closer to?

2. Can someone else do this for me?

Sometime things don't really need to be done at all. And sometimes, things need to be done, but just not by you.

You will need to prioritize those items that have to get done by you. If the majority of your business over the next five years will come from leads generated from referrals and sphere, then the "have-tos" are clear: contact and service well that group of people. Invest your time and money in that quadrant of contacts. Stay away from the nagging "to-do" list that says you need to update the expired system that you drafted two years ago and have failed to implement yet.

Next, ask some hard, frank questions of yourself and your business.

• First, can you reach your goals alone? In order to achieve the numbers you've put forward, do you need to expand your human resources?

• Second, do you need a different business model than the one you are currently using? (Told you they were hard questions!)

If you are looking to increase your production by ten percent over last year, perhaps you can obtain your goal within the status quo. But what if you are looking to double your business in couple years? Or quadruple it in five years? Is it reasonable to think that you can succeed under the same manner and with the same number of people that you have been previously?

You know the answer: undoubtedly not. As a matter of fact, this can often be the tipping point of decline or failure in a business, when you fail to realize that you, alone, cannot be chief cook and bottle washer and grow your business. A team or staff to support you may become essential when planning for your future goals The E-Myth Revisited: Why Most Small Business Don't Work and What To Do About It, by Michael Gerber, talks about this at length in his book.

It's all about the numbers today in terms of goals and in terms of human resources. Plan accordingly.

To better understand the importance of the concept of time management, take a look at how you spend you time when working. Begin with a work day and then expand your analysis to the entire week. How much time do you spend "IN" the business? This refers to the crucial everyday details of the job. It includes the showings, the opens, the listing appointments, and the negotiation of contracts. How much time do you spend on the technical aspects of the business? The accounting, the scheduling, the entering of data and working on files? Without question, this can take the lion's share of any given work day. However, danger awaits you if that is the case.

Working "ON" the business is vital if your business is to ultimately succeed and cannot be ignored. These tasks include management of the business and visionary activities. It includes mentoring, motivating, training and tracking accountability. It also includes "the big picture" activities like studying, reading, attending speakers and seminars. The problem with working ON the business is that it is too easily set aside for the daily "put out the fire" duties of tending to clients and paperwork. But that is why it is critical to create a physical time management plan that you abide as religiously as your budget. Chart it out, mark it in your Outlook calendar, and pay attention to it.

Similarly, you must think ahead in terms of the number of tasks that have to be completed to successfully make your business run. You cannot do it alone. Again, you cannot do it alone. (At least, not for very long.) If someone else can do it—delegate! If the person responsible isn't doing the job, confront the problem and replace him/her as needed. You are running a business. Without delegating responsibility, you are doomed to crash and burn. And you won't be having any fun, either.

In order to delegate, you have to have people to delegate to. Let's talk about your team. You need to have team of people to support you. The bigger your goals, the bigger your team. Team members don't have to be employees, or even traditional team members like Buyer's Agents, but you do have to surround yourself with quality people who can help you reach your goals.

The Book *The Millionaire Real Estate Agent* by Gary Keller goes into great detail on how to create a team and in what order. The Venturi Team followed this book as their bible to amazing results. I highly recommend that book for more direction as you are building your team. We will cover some of the basics here in this Chapter.

Even if you don't have a formal team, you have support around you that you should be tapping into. You have your Manager and Broker who are great at training and giving advice. You have office staff that may be able to give you some help with administrative tasks. You can also hire per transaction help from Transaction Coordinators.

Eventually, you will need to hire some administrative help. You can hire a Virtual Assistant who helps you a certain number of hours per month on marketing, database management or a variety of other things. This may be a great first step for you if you limited on space for an assistant or hours you can give them. Most VAs work for several agents and that way you don't have to guarantee part time or full time hours.

As you get busier and start making more income, you will want to bring on an administrative assistant. If you find the right person, they may eventually be your Office Manger. You want someone who can do all of the administrative, marketing and busy work you don't have time to do. Having the right admin person helps you spend time in front of prospects, which is where you can make more money. This may grow to several assistants over time.

As your business increases, you will find yourself need help with prospects. Hiring a Showing Agent or a Buyer's Agent will help reduce the time spent driving buyers all over the place. Many newer agents who don't have their own leads to work with would love to work under an experienced agent and would gladly split the commission with the lead agent for the opportunity to work with good solid leads.

As time goes buy, you may end up with several buyer's agents, a Lead Buyer Agent and a Listing Agent or tow. Again, these agents work with your leads on your team. As your business grows from your excellent marketing, repeat and referral business comes in and your excellent reputation, your team will work with you to provide the same excellent service for more and more people.

Delegating to your team is an important part of getting it all done!

How do you manage your day? How do you keep from letting the day control you?

It is important to plan everyday on paper before it begins. Spend 15 minutes in the morning, before you open your email, check Facebook messages, get out the to do lit or open the calendar and ask yourself a series of questions. The questions are something you have to come up with yourself, but they will get your mind thinking about what is important for you. Here are some sample questions:

- What can I do today bring in more leads for my Real Estate Business?

- Who do I need to follow up with today?

- What can I do today to bring me closer to finishing up a project I am working on?

- What can I do to support my team today?

- What can I do today to improve my relationship with my spouse, kids?

- What can I do today to improve my Real Estate knowledge?

- What can I do for my own personal development today?

- What cards do I need to send today?

- Who do I need to call today?

- What can I do to improve my health today?

Come up with your own list of ten questions that you will ask yourself in the morning. Your brain will answer any question you ask it. Take the time to think about them and write your answers. After you have written down the 10 answers, star the top 2. Make sure these two things get time blocked into your calendar. These are things that are important, and not just urgent. These two things will make a bigger impact on your business and your life in the long run, than 80 percent of what is on your to do list. Your brain will answer any question you ask it.

After taking the time to really think about the important things based on a series of question you created, you can then pull out your calendar and go over things you have schedule for the day. Reach out to your appointments and confirm them. Look over any meetings you have. What can you do to prepare.

After reviewing what has already been scheduled, take out your Master Project List and your to do list. Your Master Project list is a living document that you created when you did your yearly planning. You should review this document and the main projects daily. Is there anything you need to schedule today to get done off this list? Then review your to do list. After the import things are schedule, review the to do list for things you can delegate or delete. Also not anything that you need to do today and make sure they are time blocked, or scheduled in your calendar. Things that are scheduled get done.

Another tip for managing your activity is to not over schedule your day. Really think about how long something will take, including prep time and drive time if needed. You should also consider leaving "white" space on your calendar. Instead of scheduling for the entire hour, schedule for 50 minutes. This will give you time to get up and stretch, grab a snack or return a phone call.

Focus on what is most important, the rest will get done, or not. We are all busy. Every Real Estate Agent I know has more to do in a day than can possibly get done. Set your intentions at the start of the day, time block and adjust and reschedule, as you need to. If it doesn't get done today, it will get done tomorrow. Or not. Remember, it is about time choices, not time management. *Happy choosing!*

Following Through To
Achieve Your Goals

In the very first chapter of this book we talked about Goal Setting, creating a plan to Revamp your Real Estate Business and have your best year every as a Realtor. Now, in this final chapter, we are going to talk about Goal Achievement.

Goal Setting and Goal Achievement are related, but not the same thing. I think Goal Setting is the number one thing you can to in order to have an extraordinary business. Goal Achievement however will not happen if you don't handle these 3 important aspects of Goal Achievement.

I am going to tell you what they are, and they will sound so simple. I know they did to me the first time I heard them. You are almost there; follow through to the end of this chapter to fully understand what we mean.

In order to achieve anything you want you must manage your Inner Game, Your Outer Game and Your Action. I believe that 80% is Inner Game, 10% is Outer Game and 10% is action. That is a big claim. Maybe it is 60/20/20, either way; your Inner Game, in my opinion, is the most important aspect of Goal Achievement.

Let's start with the other two first. What do we mean by Outer Game? Your Outer Game is your Skill Set. This could be your Sales Skills, your

Script Writing Skills, or Negotiating Skills. They are the skills you need to master in order to become a great Real Estate Agent. What can you do, learn or master to improve your Outer Game?

Tony Robbins talks about a concept called CANI, Constant And Never-ending Improvement. You can use this concept to examine everything you do as a Real Estate Agent and Examine where you may need to work on your Outer Game. How was the Listing Presentation? What could you have done to improve the Contract Negotiations on the last Purchase Agreement you presented? What could you do to improve the script you are using to book an appointment with the Expired Lead you just called on? By analyzing your process, outcomes and skills, you are improving your Outer Game.

Skills sound like a major contributor to success! If the Outer Game is only 10 to 20 percent of Goal Achievement, what are the other two about?

Action! Ready, Set, ACTION! Action is doing the business!

Some agents are great students. They go to all the classes, take all the seminars, and have all the designations such as GRI and ABR and even ALHS, but they don't apply the knowledge. They are studying, learning and practicing, yet they do not get out there and work the business. Don't get me wrong, I am a huge fan of personal fan of personal development and business development training, but there comes a time when you need to put that training into ACTION!

Some Real Estate Agents, especially when they first start in this industry, are thrilled to "be their own boss" or are happy to "make their own schedule." Sometimes, without goals and deadlines to keep you in action, you spend too much time sleeping in, at the beach with kids, or playing golf with potential prospects. Accountability in the form of Coaching or even an Accountability Partner can help keep you focused on a daily and weekly basis and help keep you in action!

An Accountability Partner can be another Real Estate Agent, or someone in a different profession. It is important to find someone you can depend on to be on the phone calls or to report numbers via email as you agree upon. This isn't about one person 'coaching' another; it is about you being accountable to someone to do what you say you are going to do. Knowing you have to tell a person you didn't finish what you said you would or didn't hit your goal will help motivate you to do more!

If you are not reaching your goals, is it because you are not good at what you do, Outer Game? Or because you are not taking enough Action? I am sure those two areas play a part in not achieving goals for many real estate agents out there. However, I am going to suggest, based on the thousands of real estate agents I have worked with over the years and seeing so many agents, especially new agents fail in the first two years, that the most important thing to master in order to achieve your goals, is your Inner Game.

The main thing that keeps us from getting what we want out of our real Estate business and out of life is the story in our mind as to why we don't have it. The Inner Game is all about Mindset!

The story in your mind will become the story of our life. Athletes know this. They understand that preparing for a game or a race mentally, is just as important as preparing physically. They are going over the race in their mind over and over and over. They see themselves crossing the finish line or the goal line. They see themselves winning. The story in their mind becomes the story of their life.

What is your story?

What do you tell yourself about Goal Achievement? What are your stories about your Real Estate Career? Maybe your story is that it is hard to find leads? Maybe your story is that Buyers are Liars, or that you don't have the experience to work with luxury home sellers. If you change your story to "I am the top producing agent at my office" or "I am running a Real Estate Team that closes over 20 Million Dollars in Production," your brain would be focus on what it could do to make it true. Your subconscious mind wants to prove you right, whatever you say, positive or negative. So why would you be putting negative stories out there?

Sometimes you don't even realize that your brain is filled with negative stories. 87% of everything out there in the world is negative so it is important to guard against the negativity as much as we can. Limit the news you are watching, especially right before bed and first thing in the morning. Instead, concentrate on reading something positive that will build you up and help your mind stay focused on the positives and on helping you achieve your goals.

Repeating your goals as I AM statements, positively stating your goals in the present tense as though you have already achieved them will help your mind stay positive. I AM making $100,000 from my Real Estate Business this year. I AM listing at least two houses per month. I AM the top team in the entire Miami Area.

What are you doing to visualize your goals? What are you doing to visualize your success? It is important to prepare mentally for all of your Real Estate Goals. Picture yourself winning that company award, walk through giving that perfect listing presentation, and visualize achieving the income goals and moving into your dream house or driving your dream car.

Exercise those dream-building muscles. You may need to test drive that dream car of yours, or tour that dream house you want your family to live in. Put up pictures that you can look at that will remind you of your goals and dreams. You have to exercise those dream-building muscles.

Give your goals deadlines and schedule them into your calendar. Schedule that dream trip with your kids, put the date on the calendar you want to do car shopping, and set appointments for getting your hair done before the annual awards banquet at your company when you will be receiving your awards!

In setting your goals, we talked a little about figuring out your "WHY."

WHY do you want to hit goals? Your WHY may be your family, your spouse, your team. You may want to be able to contribute to a certain charity or organization. Don't forget your WHY. Your WHY will help drive you to do the things you need to everyday in your business. If your WHY is big enough, you will get through any HOW!

Schedule your time wisely like we talked about in the previous chapter. Distractions will come at you and will pull you off of the important things you must to do reach your goals. Don't let those little things like email, Social Media, nagging sellers, or other Realtors; distract you from your plan and your goals. Your goals are too big and too important to be pulled away from.

Sometimes the distractions are coming from our head. I heard a trainer once refer to it as the "Border Patrol" in your head. We have borders in our mind that are at the end of our comfort zone. Whenever we try something new, or talk to someone who intimidates us, we are pushing up against our boards. Our sub conscious mind wants to help protect us, so it tries to stop us as we reach the end of our comfort zone.

Sometimes the voices in our head are screaming so loud, that we shut down, stop trying and give up on goals we have set. We use the excuse that the goal was too big, or that it was unrealistic, or too hard. We convince our self that it is okay to lower the goal to something more attainable.

Don't listen to that voice! That voice that is trying to protect you is actually keeping you stuck. By not pushing up against the borders of your comfort zone you are staying right where you are now. Your brain might even be telling you "things are really not bad where I am at. I am doing better than most, I should just be satisfied."

If you listen to that voice, if you let it shut you down and let it keep you playing small, you will never reach your full potential. When you notice the voice and recognize that you are settling and playing small, fight back. Thank your brain for trying to protect you, but let it know that you got this, that you can do more than you are doing now and will. Thank it for sharing, then push through the uncomfortable feeling. You CAN do it. You have a plan and will succeed. You deserve to be the best you can be. The client's you can help get into their dream home deserve you to be the best you can be. The team members who will be joining you on this journey deserve the best YOU that you can be.

In fact, hearing those focuses trying to protect you and keep you playing small is not what should alarm you. NOT hearing those voices in your head should be the warning sign that you are not living up to your full potential, that you are playing too small.

Keep expanding your vision and your options. Get around other top producing agents so you can expand your ideas about what is possible.

Go to events like NAR and your local Association Events. It is important to get away from your local bubble and expand your mind to the possibilities that are out there in this great profession.

Hire a coach.

Everyone should have at least one coach in his or her life. Find someone who will push you, stretch you, help you become more than even you can fathom right now. A good coach will see potential in you that even you don't realize is there. The investment in the right coach will help you get farther faster than you realize.

Isn't now your time to really step into your greatness and achieve those goals?

If not, then when?

You are part of an amazing profession, one that allows you to create the business and the income you want. You don't have to settle, or to only earn what someone else has determined you are worth. YOU are in charge of your business, your income, your goals.

Take the things we have talked about here and Revamp your real estate business, Revamp your goal, and *Revamp your life!*

Conclusion

Even though this is a relatively small book, it is chock full of so many ideas that you may feel your head is going to explode. So where do you start?

Our intention which writing this is for you to walk away with a least one great idea that you will go ahead and implement. Baby steps. Then once you've implemented that idea, move to the next.

You do not have to do it all yourself, either. You are not on a deserted island with only a volleyball to talk to. You have resources and talented people available to you which even if not free can help you quickly implement each and every strategy so that they are done, and done right. This will leave you with the benefit of these strategies working for you and giving you leverage to make the most of every day.

With the steep climb of technology happening daily, you can't afford to sit back and watch other agents embrace changes in how to market yourself with you watching from the wings.

Think of your mobile device. Is there a reason you are not still using a Palm or Blackberry that was state-of-the-art when you first bought it?

Why did you buy a new iPhone or Droid phone just two or three years after you bought your last one? It's because technology marches on and you want to take advantage of all the advances that it can bring you and not be left behind while your competition enjoys the benefits of staying current.

So, are you ready to step up and be seen, be known and be heard?

Are you ready to do the simple steps that it takes to share your knowledge and be acknowledged as an expert in your field?

Are you plain sick and tired of being too busy all the time and not changing how you do things?

A lot of people are depending on you. Your spouse, your kids, even your friends. They are wanting to share their life with you and for you to be happy, healthy and present. With some thought and planning and the willingness to change, you truly can live the life of your dreams.

Thank you for reading *Agent Revamp*. It was a labor of love and we'd like to hear from you.

As time produces new technologies, ideas and inspirations, we will be updating this book and we want to keep you in the conversation.

Register for FREE Book Updates, Agent Training, and other Bonus content at www.AgentRevamp.com/register

At our website, you can also request a no-obligation Career Assessment, Website Analysis or Sales Scripting Coaching Session to see how you might benefit from making changes so this next year will be your best year.

AGENT REVAMP

About The Authors

Brett Miller

Brett Miller is the Founder and President of HoopJumper LLC, a marketing, training and Internet technology company for real estate professionals. Brett has been creating Internet websites for businesses since the dawn of the industry in 1994.

Prior to his transition to Internet Technologies, Brett finished top of his class at his computer graphics technical college. Fresh out of college, Brett opened his first business and was featured as the Spotlight Business for his local Chamber of Commerce. This led to him being hired to help launch the computer graphics department of a major Southern California printing and publishing company who was transitioning into the digital age.

In 1994, Brett was an original beta tester for Adobe's Page Mill, the first consumer software for creating websites. Mastering this skill, Brett was quickly hired by a local Internet Service Provider in Southern California to become their first Director of Website Development.

Soon after, Brett was recruited to create the Website division for the nation's #1 niche advertising agency specializing in real estate agent branding and marketing, which he grew into the second most profitable non-seminar department in the company.

In 2005, Brett Miller co-founded HoopJumper with the mantra of "We jump through hoops so you won't have to." With a focus on personal service, creative flair, and treating each client uniquely, HoopJumper saw its business grow in an era when other companies had to fold up shop.

HoopJumper celebrated its 10th anniversary in 2015. After a full decade of building the best real estate agent websites in the industry under Brett's leadership, HoopJumper now integrates all aspects of internet and social media marketing, and showing busy real estate agents how to harness the world wide web to become their technology partner and help them make more money.

Cheri Alguire

Cheri Alguire is a Business Coach who has partnered with over a thousand Small Business Owners, Network Marketers, and Real Estate Professionals including agents, owners, brokers, managers, assistants, loan officers and title closers, and busy super-moms to help them become more successful in business and in life.

Known throughout the business world as "Coach Cheri," she is the author of six business planning guides which have helped struggling agents up to million dollar earners create their annual business plan and help them consistently have better more successful years every year.

"Coach Cheri's Business Planning Guides" now have editions for Real Estate Agents, Real Estate Managers and Brokers, Real Estate Team Members, Real Estate Investors, Small Business Owners and Network Marketing Professionals.

As an experienced entrepreneur with a background in real estate and owning small businesses, Cheri Alguire knows how frustrating it can be to keep working harder and harder and still fall short of your desired results. Her unique individualized approach to coaching makes her stand out from the crowd.

Known as an engaging presenter, Cheri enjoys speaking to and working with groups large or small, including Real Estate Offices and Associations, Business Groups, Running Groups, Coaching Groups, Adventure Groups, RVing Groups, Mastermind Groups, Women's Groups, and Non-Profit Organizations.

Cheri Alguire is also the co-Founder and CEO of HoopJumper, LLC, a marketing, training and Internet technology company for real estate professionals, where her focus on what really works for real estate agents has supplied a needed "real world" dimension to the many advanced technological solutions.

For more information on Cheri Alguire please visit www.CheriAlguire.com or visit her Amazon author page at www.Amazon.com/author/cherialguire

AGENT REVAMP

Eric Lofholm

Eric Lofholm is a Master Sales Trainer who has taught his proven sales systems to thousands of professionals around the world. He is President and CEO of Eric Lofholm International, Inc., an organization he founded to professionally train people on the art and science of selling.

Eric began his career as a sales failure. At his first sales job he was put on quota probation after failing to meeting the minimum quota two months in a row. It was at this point that Eric met his sales mentor. After being professionally trained by a Sales Coach, Eric not only achieved his sales quota, he eventually become the top producer at that company. Studying the science of selling, Eric became a sales master and went on to become the top producer at two more companies prior to starting Eric Lofholm International.

Eric is a naturally gifted teacher. For over 15 years Eric has been sharing his proven sales increasing ideas with people all over the world.

Eric believes that selling equals service. He also believes in working towards mastery of the fundamentals of lead generation, appointment setting, and delivering a high quality presentation.

Eric Lofholm is the author of:

- The System: The Proven 3-Step Formula Anyone Can Learn to Get More Leads, Book More Appointments, and Make More Money
- Sales Scripting Mastery: The 7-Step System for Consistently Delivering Successful Sales Presentations
- Duplication: The Key to Creating Freedom in Your Network Marketing Business
- Focus: The Key Skill to Igniting Your Productivity So You Can Get More Done Everyday
- Bulls Eye: The Step-By-Step Process of The Most Powerful Goal Setting Process to Achieving Any Goal
- 21 Ways to Close More Sales Now

For more information on Eric Lofholm please visit www.EricLofholm.com or visit his Amazon author page at www.Amazon.com/author/ericlofholm

Register for Free Updates & Bonus Content

Get access to exclusive bonus content, be notified when new real estate agent training audio, video and other resources are available, as well as free book updates as they happen.

.AgentRevamp.com/register

Grow To Greatness Publishing

www.ingramcontent.com/pod-product-compliance
Lightning Source LLC
Chambersburg PA
CBHW060618210326
41520CB00010B/1384